The
SACRED HEART
OF CHRIST

The SACRED HEART OF CHRIST

Spiritual Readings

BY

REV. F. KONZ, O.M.I.

BENZIGER BROTHERS

NEW YORK, CHICAGO, CINCINNATI, SAN FRANCISCO

BENZIGER BROTHERS

PRINTERS TO THE HOLY APOSTOLIC SEE

1936

Imprimatur:

✠ H. J. MEYSING, O.M.I.
Vicar of Missions

KIMBERLEY (SOUTH AFRICA), EPIPHANY, 1934

INTRODUCTION

No one can know another by his appearance, his dress, his words, even his deeds. We do not know anyone until we know his heart. It is then and only then that we can be truly said to know anyone. Among casual acquaintances this knowledge is most difficult to attain: hence people remain forever casual acquaintances. It is generally sorrow that brings out heart knowledge; any other emotion is too ineffective to disclose the nature and affections of the heart. But sorrow will almost always open up the sealed casket of the heart: witness the numberless friendships that began in illness, misfortune, affliction and the tearing of the heart.

How frequently it is true that Christ does not seem to know some soul or other who knows neither Christ nor sorrow. And yet how intimate He is with the soul that sorrows. Were you or I to be suddenly afflicted with an overpowering cross beyond our own carrying, to whom would we go for assistance and for someone to help us carry a dire cross? To an enemy of long standing, to someone who long ago disdained us, to an unknown man or woman? I think not! Naturally, we would have recourse to a friend of long standing, to one who for years and time after time has proved his affection, friendship and love for us. Is this not so? It is most assuredly true in Christ's dealings with the men and women of the world for many generations past. When Christ has some severe cross to give out, a cross that must be carried as He carried the first cross to Calvary, whom does He ask to carry that cross? Does He ask an enemy, or someone who for years has been flaunting the laws of God in His face, or a stranger who does not even know Him? Just as we would go in insufferable agony to a life-long friend, so, too, does Christ seek out His friends when He has crosses to carry. Very seldom does He ask His enemies to suffer! But He still says to His friends, "Take up your cross and come and follow Me."

We cannot know Christ and Christ cannot know us unless we mutually know each other's hearts. And to know Christ is simply to love Him. Once we know His heart, we must, as night follows the day, love Him. And the more we know Him, the better and deeper is our love.

Reverend Father Konz, O.M.I., in this estimable work *The Heart of Christ* reveals the intimacies and the generosity of the Sacred Heart in a vivid portrayal of Gospel fact, abstaining from the usual sentimentality. Some pages, I believe to be inspired for certain souls; some chapters will captivate every reader, some paragraphs will move mountains of apparently impassable obstacles to a genuine love of Christ.

For many reasons, I rejoice that the Spiritual Book Associates has been fortunate enough to select this book. Is it merely accidental that an African missioner should give us our spiritual inspiration for June, the month of the Sacred Heart? To my mind, it is a direct message from the Heart of Christ in the heart of Africa. The standard of the Spiritual Book Associates has from its inception been "UT COGNOSCANT TE;" "that they may know Thee the one true God and Him whom Thou hast sent, Jesus Christ." The purpose of this large group associated for spiritual reading is to select a broad *Christology*, from any and every angle that will serve to make Him known. That one project accomplished, love is sure to follow. Quite appropriately, therefore, Father Konz has chosen to open up the secrets of the Sacred Heart, without a knowledge of which we could never know the real, the inner Christ, the God-Man, whose Heart sheds a new light on a new facet on what He did and said. We may well note here that it took centuries of unrequited love before Christ complained to St. Margaret Mary Alacoque, not indeed that the world remained unappreciative of His power, or of His infinite perfection, or that men and women of the world failed to notice His mercy or His omniscience, but merely the plaintive cry of a broken heart, "Behold this heart that has loved so much." To contemplate His mercy that is above all His works, to marvel at His omnipotence, to draw back in fear at the miracle of His ubiquity is a wholesome thing, but must needs end in a sort of academic bewilderment; but when we know His breathing, pulsing, throbbing Heart, we see infinitely more clearly the outstanding attributes of God and His infinite perfections.

To think of the mercy of God is a vast concept. But when we see it vividly acted out in the life of a Man who is also God, how much more significance it bears. When we see Christ writing secret sins in the pliable sands, and one accuser after another fleeing away in shame, turning to the woman with all touch of hatred of hypocrisy gone from His voice, and asking, "Does no one accuse you?"—and on the answer, "No man, Lord," with a still finer majestic finality in His voice, He says to her, "Go in peace and sin no more," then the vast idea of God's mercy becomes a tangible thing that even the dull of heart can see and understand.

The omnipotence of God is so far beyond the ordinary human comprehension. Not so when we see fear-stricken fishermen in a storm-tossed craft, shaking the weary, sleeping Christ until He is aroused. Not so, when we see the white-robed figure arise undauntedly in a sinking ship and, raising a commanding hand in the blackness of the night, say to the winds and waves and waters of Galilee, "Peace, be still." And the apostles with open, wondering eyes, bewildered, asking each other, "What manner of man is this?"

When we see Christ lifting from His prayerful knees a beseeching father and saying, "Go in peace, thy son liveth," we begin to know what we mean when we say that God is everywhere.

What can the love of God signify to us until we see Christ raising to life the daughter of Jairus, curing by the way the woman afflicted with the loss of blood, Magdalen, the supreme proof of a God-Man's love, Christ and the lepers, Christ and the children and a hundred other instances that reveal God's love and Christ's Sacred Heart that so loved me. But, above all, it is on Calvary, when the sacred lips are sealed and the sacred eyes are closed, when the Heart is open for the world still to look within, that we realize how intensely He did love.

Catholics and non-Catholics will extend a cordial welcome to this book.

Again I say that Father Konz has produced a worth-while book that will go far towards achieving the ideal, "UT COGNOSCANT TE."

FRANCIS X. DOWNEY, S. J.,
Editorial Secretary,
Spiritual Book Associates.

Preface

THE Devotion to the Sacred Heart presents to us Jesus Christ all amiable and loving. "Having loved His own who were in the world, He loved them unto the end" (John 13, 1). The object of this devotion is to return love for love. The reciprocation of love is its peculiar characteristic. We cannot fail to observe that Our Saviour's excessive love is despised and rejected by many. The worship of the Sacred Heart is therefore very appropriate for our time, the stigma of which is called inordinate self-love. The more we know the riches and treasures of this devotion, the more we shall be convinced that nothing can be more efficacious to make us love God with all our heart, soul, mind and strength than the devotion to the Sacred Heart.

It cannot be the object of this book to exhaust the infinite riches of the Heart of Our Saviour, it wishes merely to point out a way of rendering them fruitful for the spiritual advancement of our souls. If these pages should contribute to the propagation of the kingdom of the Sacred Heart in the lives of the children of the Church, the author will feel that the Sacred Heart has blessed them.

CONTENTS

CONTENTS

Chapter I

HEART OF JESUS, SON OF THE ETERNAL
FATHER

GOD is light and love. All the other attributes of God which we enumerate are expressions by which we eliminate from the essence of God imperfections which our feeble understanding might be inclined to attach to Him. When we say, for instance, that God is almighty, we mean to say that His will cannot be opposed by anything, so that He can do what He wills. When we say God is eternal, we mean to say that God is not circumscribed by time. But when we say that God is light, or love, we do not eliminate anything imperfect from God. Light and love are expressions which refer to God's nature as it is in itself, and not in its relations to created things.

St. John says: "God is charity" (1 John 4, 8). God not only has love, God not only is able to love, but He is love; God and love are identical things. Since God is the supreme Good, and since only good things are lovable, it follows that God's love must be immense and infinite, because there is no greater lovable good than Himself.

It is in the nature of good things to communicate their inherent good qualities to other beings. A good man will always love his neighbor, that is to say, he communicates his goodness to others by kind thoughts and good deeds. If this is true of creatures, it must certainly be true of that furnace of love which is God. That God has communicated, and still communicates, His goodness to others, we know in the first place from the creation of the world. The world around us is nothing else but a striking manifestation of the love of God, because God's goodness and perfections are copied in God's creatures in a thousandfold manner. But this is not the only divine manifestation of God's love and goodness. God went a step further. Though His infinite love moved Him to create the world and to communicate His goodness to creatures, yet He deigned to speak to man as a friend to his friend. Hence St. Paul writes: "God, who, at sundry times, and in divers manners, spoke in times past to the fathers by the prophets, last of all, in these days hath spoken to us by His Son" (Hebrews 1, 1-2).

It was by way of supernatural revelation that God manifested to us His goodness and immense love for us. In divers manners He spoke to mankind, that is, in such a way that the truth of His love became more and more evident, and its proofs more and more tangible, until they reached their culminating point in the Incarnation of the Son of God. St. John clothes this fact in these words: "God so loved the world as to give His only-begotten Son" (3,16). The greatness of the love of God for us consists in this, that He sent not a servant, not an angel, but His only-begotten Son.

Since it is the wish of the Church that we should venerate the Heart of Jesus as a symbol of love, she introduces to us, in the Litany of the Sacred Heart, this Heart as the Heart of Jesus, Son of the Eternal Father. It is not difficult to see that these words are to perpetuate the grandest proof of God's love for us, and to bring home to us that the Sacred Heart itself is a memorial forever reminding us of three elements which constitute the Mystery of the Incarnation of the Son of God. It is a memorial, not of stone, not of metal, not a manuscript; no, it is the physical, living Heart of Our Saviour as a symbol of love. And these three elements are: The love and generosity of God the Father, of the Eternal Father, who gave away His only Son; secondly, the love and generosity of God the Son, who willingly sacrificed Himself for us; and, thirdly, the love of Father and Son centralized and stored up as it were in the Sacred Heart present on the altars of our churches.

Therefore when we say: "Heart of Jesus, Son of the Eternal Father," we are reminded of the Eternal love of the Eternal Father as shown in the Incarnation. The Eternal Father's love for us is as old as God Himself. "I have loved thee with an everlasting love," says He through the prophet Jeremias, "therefore have I drawn thee, taking pity on thee" (31, 3). The Eternal Father's love for us is as tender as that of a mother's. For He says through the prophet Isaias: "Can a woman forget her infant so as not to have pity on the son of her womb? And if she should forget, yet will not I forget thee. Behold, I have graven thee in My hands" (49,

15-16). The eternal Father's love for us is also unselfish. For St. Paul writes: "God commendeth His charity toward us because, when as yet we were sinners, ... Christ died for us" (Romans 5, 8-9). The love of the Eternal Father is longsuffering, patient and kind. "The Lord is compassionate and merciful, longsuffering and plenteous in mercy" (Psalm 102, 8). "He hath not dealt with us according to our sins, nor rewarded us according to our iniquities" (Psalm 102, 10). The eternal love of the Eternal Father is also heroic: "God so loved the world as to give His only-begotten Son (John 3, 16).

Jesus Christ is the Son of the Eternal Father, and if ever son was like to his father, it is Jesus Christ, the Son of the Eternal Father. For, as St. Paul says: Jesus Christ is "the brightness of His Father's glory, and the figure of His substance" (Hebrews 1, 3). It is this Son's Heart which we are to adore and love. Who can doubt that in this Heart there dwelt the love of the Eternal Father? And Our Lord's own personal love for us, could it in any way differ from that of His Father's? Are not Christ and His Father one? Therefore Our Lord's love for us also had to be eternal. And so it was. For at the Last Supper, "having loved His own who were in the world, He loved them unto the end" (John 13, 1). This love of His was as tender as a mother's when He said in the desert: "I have compassion on the people"; or when He asked the woman taken in adultery: "Woman, hath no man condemned thee? . . . Neither will I condemn thee. Go and now sin no more" (*Ib.* 8, 10-11). Our Lord's love was unselfish. "My meat," He says, "is to do the will of Him that sent Me, that I may perfect His work" (*Ib.* 4, 34). Our Lord's love is long-suffering, patient and kind: He leaves the ninety-nine sheep in the desert and goes after the one that is lost, and when He has found it, carries it home on His shoulders. Our Lord's love is heroic: He is the Good Shepherd who giveth His life for His sheep, as He actually did on the cross.

Behold, then, the immense love of Father and Son which brought about the great work of the redemption of the world. And now our eyes are fixed on the Heart of which it is said that it is the Heart of the Son of the Eternal Father. It is not any heart, it is not any love which is contained therein, it is the Heart of a Son whose Father loved us so much that He gave away His Son for us; hence it is a Heart in which we find combined the love of Father and Son so that we can say that the Sacred Heart is God's own way of love. When we say God's way of love, we mean to say, that God means the worship of the Sacred Heart to be a touchstone of our faith in the Incarnation of His Son.

St. John says that he cannot be a disciple of Jesus Christ who denies the Incarnation. Now, the Sacred Heart, the physical, living Heart of Our Lord is presented to us as a symbol of that love which was revealed by, and in, the Incarnation. Therefore, how can a man believe in the great love revealed by the Incarnation if he does not love and worship the Sacred Heart? Such a man has not yet realized that the love of God has its origin in God Himself, and that this love is centralized, and condensed, as it were, in that Heart which is both human and divine; and because it is the Heart of God, we must give it divine worship. To act otherwise would be rank heresy, and to neglect this worship would be a cruel offence against that excess of love which was revealed by the Incarnation. But whoever will worship this Heart will find that this devotion is like a book which interprets the mystery of the Incarnation. It will tell Him about the love of the Father who sacrificed His Son, above the love of the Son who sacrificed Himself, and it will tell him about that immense love which still burns in the Sacred Heart present on our altars. The knowledge of the Sacred Heart will be to him a compendium of the science of God; he who knows the Sacred Heart knows God; he who loves the Sacred Heart loves God; and he whose heart is like to the Sacred Heart is like to God, a son of God, and an heir to heaven.

Chapter II

HEART OF JESUS, FORMED BY THE HOLY GHOST
IN THE WOMB OF THE VIRGIN MOTHER

THOUGH a human heart, the origin and the home of the Sacred Heart were not of this world. This heart is the Heart of the Son of the Eternal Father. But the Eternal Father had decreed from all eternity that His Son was to take His human body from the Virgin Mary. In the fulness of time the Archangel Gabriel was sent by God to Mary in Nazareth, with the sublime message: "Fear not, Mary, for thou hast found grace with God. Behold, thou shalt conceive in thy womb, and shalt bring forth a Son; and thou shalt call His name Jesus" (Luke 1, 30-31). "And Mary said to the angel: How shall this be done, because I know not man? And the angel, answering, said to her: The Holy Ghost shall come upon thee, and the power of the Most High shall overshadow thee. And therefore also the Holy which shall be born of theee shall be called the Son of God. . . . And Mary said: Behold the handmaid of the Lord; be it done unto me according to thy word" (*Ib*. 1, 34, 35, 38). These words of the Evangelist inform us of the origin and the home of the Sacred Heart. The Sacred Heart was formed by the Holy Ghost, in the womb of the Virgin Mary.

The forming of the Sacred Heart is attributed and appropriated to the operation of the Holy Ghost. Since the forming of the Sacred Heart is an immediate operation of the Holy Ghost, and therefore of God Himself, a human origin is thereby emphatically excluded. Once St. John wrote in his gospel: "As many as received Christ, He gave them power to be made the sons of God, to them that believe in His name, who are born, not of blood, nor of the will of the flesh, nor of the will of man, but of God" (1, 12, 13). It is the children of God that St. John speaks of, and he says that the children of God are not born of any human marriage, but they are made children of God by the sole creative power of God. In a similar way the Sacred Heart owes its origin, not to any human parent; it is the creative power of the Holy Ghost that formed the Sacred Heart. It is the same Spirit of whom Holy Scripture says that "the Spirit of God moved over the waters" (Genesis 1, 3). It is, as it were, the personal creative will of God, who as a creating, forming, vivifying power rules and governs everything, pervades and penetrates everything. In fine, it is God Himself who made this Heart. In being formed by the Holy Ghost, this Heart received from the Holy Spirit not only its existence, but also the unction of created santification.

Since the Sacred Heart is to reveal the love of God, it is not to be wondered at that the Holy Ghost should have sanctified it. For the Holy Ghost is the personal love of Father and Son. If it is true that "the charity of God is poured forth in our hearts by the Holy Ghost who is given to us" (Romans 5, 5), then it must certainly be true that the Holy Ghost poured forth the love of God in the Sacred Heart. The love of God is a love of friendship by which we will and desire for God all good things for His own sake. Since this love is an unselfish love, and since the fulness of this love was poured forth in the Sacred Heart, it is evident that the love of the Sacred Heart was unselfish in the highest degree. It was pure, it was not mercenary, it was not the love of hirelings. The Holy Ghost, the Third Person of the Blessed Trinity, dwells in this Heart, and there He pours forth the charity of God, that is sanctifying grace. And since the Holy Ghost dwells in this Heart, it is encompassed and penetrated by the perfections of the Holy Ghost. Holiness, justice, charity, mercy, truth, compassion and all the other virtues dwell in the Sacred Heart. "God is charity," says St. John, "and he that abideth in charity, abideth in God, and God in him" (1 John 4, 16). The Sacred Heart is full of God, the fulness of the love of God dwells in it, and it is adorned with an immensity of grace. And then the Holy Ghost infused in the Sacred Heart His seven gifts, seven powers, as it were, to bring our faith, hope and charity into action. Needless to say that in the Sacred Heart, hope and charity are always in action, because Our Saviour always hoped and desired vehemently the redemption of the world, and Our Saviour always loved God and man. But instead of the gift of faith, Our Lord possessed the gift of the Beatific Vision. He always saw God face to face.

The Holy Ghost, then, is the origin of the Sacred Heart, forming it in a twofold way, namely, by giving it existence, and filling it with the love of God. And this was done in the womb of the Virgin Mother, Our Blessed Lady. The womb of the Virgin Mother is the home of the Sacred Heart. Mary is the Mother of Jesus Christ. As He took from her His body, so also He took from her His Sacred Heart. When we say that the Sacred Heart was formed by the Holy Ghost in the womb of the Virgin Mother, we seem immediately to imply that the Sacred Heart inherited all the good qualities of the Immaculate Heart of Mary.

Mary's heart was solely devoted to the love and service of God. Her heart was a holy temple of God. For "Holiness becometh Thy house, O Lord, unto length of days," says Holy Scripture (Psalm 92, 5). The heart of Mary was adorned with all the holiness and glory becoming the house of God. She was full of grace, and never was she stained by any sin whatsoever. Hence the Heart of her Son could be only holy, since it could not be stained by original sin, and from the very beginning she devoted the Sacred Heart to the love and service of God.

The heart of Mary was also a temple that was never violated or destroyed by sin. Her heart was not a playground for worldly thoughts and desires; it was a place where Mary met God in sweet prayer. Not the least shadow of sin entered into Mary's heart, because it was always in perfect keeping with the will of God. The Sacred Heart also is a temple shining and glittering with the gold of grace and virtues. The world and sin have no access to this Heart; this Heart is a heart of prayer which used to spend whole nights in prayer, and even now prays for us incessantly in the Blessed Sacrament. This Heart is in perfect keeping with the will of God, and its meat is to do the will of God.

Mary's heart was also an altar where she daily offered herself to God in perfect humility. Did not the Sacred Heart become a perfect holocaust for us? Christ "emptied Himself," says the Apostle, "taking the form of a servant, being made in the likeness of men, and in habit found as a man. He humbled Himself, becoming obedient unto death, even to the death of the cross" (Philippians 2, 7-8).

Lastly, Mary's heart was a sacrifice. She

faithfully kept the word of God in her heart, and thereby made her life a perfect sacrifice. For, by obeying the word of God, she submitted her will to the divine will, and recognized God as her Lord and Master. What sacrifices did the Sacred Heart not make for us? This Heart sacrificed money and earthly goods by becoming poor in the stable of Bethlehem. Moved by this heart's love, Our Lord sacrificed comfort and ease by wandering about in Palestine and preaching to the people. Moved by this Heart, He gave away His body to be buffeted, His life to be delivered to an unjust judge; His good name to be calumniated; the limbs of His body to be nailed to the cross; His strength to death; even the last drop of His blood He shed because He wanted to sacrifice Himself for us in a perfect manner.

Since, then, the Sacred Heart was formed in the womb of Mary, who else but Mary could better help us to enter into the spirit of the devotion to the Sacred Heart. She is the Mother of the Sacred Heart, and therefore knows all its beauties, all its perfections, all its glories. Therefore through Mary is the royal road to the Sacred Heart of her Son.

Chapter III

SACRED HEART OF JESUS, SUBSTANTIALLY
UNITED TO THE WORD OF GOD

IN ORDER to grasp the full import of these words, it will be good to remember again and again, that the object of the devotion to the Sacred Heart is the Heart of flesh of Our Lord taken from the substance of His Blessed Mother, symbolizing and manifesting the infinite and eternal love of God. This Heart is substantially united to the Word of God. St. John says: "The Word was made flesh, and dwelt among us; and we saw His glory, the glory as it were of the Only-begotten of the Father" (1, 14). The Word of God is nobody else than the Second Person of the Blessed Trinity, the Son of God. Therefore the Word of God is a Divine Person, who has been existing from all eternity. Now, this Divine Person became flesh; that is, became man. He took to Himself a human soul and a human body. The Athanasian Creed informs us how this was done. It says that Our Lord assumed the human nature to His Divine nature; that is, He took on the human nature in addition to His Divine nature in such a way that though there are two natures in Jesus Christ, yet there is only one Person, the Divine Person of the Eternal Son of God. This assumption of the human nature was the work of the Blessed Trinity; the Father and the Holy Ghost assisted in the work of the Incarnation, but it was only the Son, or the Word, who became Man.

But how are the two natures united into one Person? Here we must be on our guard that we may avoid erroneous conceptions. The divine and the human nature could not be united in such a way that the human nature became the divine nature, or that the divine nature became the human nature, because a finite being cannot become an infinite being, nor can an infinite being become finite. Neither could they be united in this way that the divine nature lost something and the human nature acquired something, because the divine nature cannot be altered or changed. From this it follows that the two natures in Christ are united in such a way that in Christ these two natures are distinct and perfect—neither changed nor confused. It is a union of which we find no analogy in created things, and therefore it is called by the theologians the hypostatic union; that is, such a union exists between the two natures in Jesus Christ that the Second Person of God is also truly Man.

In the light of this doctrine it becomes clear that, when we say that the Sacred Heart is substantially united to the Word of God, we mean to say that it is the Heart of God. The Sacred Heart, this Heart of flesh and taken from the substance of the Mother of God, enters upon a unique relationship to the Word of God. The human Heart of Jesus Christ was united to the eternal love and charity of God and, by virtue of this union, all the ardor and love of God was there, and all the fervor and tenderness of man. The foundation of this relationship is the human love of the Sacred Heart. Two loves are united because two natures are united. But though there are two loves, yet there is only one who loves, and He is the Eternal Word. Father and mother love their child. There are two loves, but also two persons who love. Father and mother are united, but only from an exterior reason; it is the child that united them. Our Lord loves us with two loves, but there is only one Person who loves, and it was not we that united these two loves, but Our Lord assumed a human heart, and remained one Person. If, then, there are two loves in Jesus Christ and only one Person, it is impossible that the human love of Jesus Christ could be independent of His divine love. That this human love is not independent is no imperfection. For, being substantially united to the Word of God, the Sacred Heart was elevated and raised beyond the limits of its own love; it was lifted above the order of creation; it was united to a Divine Person, became the Heart of God and was thereby deified. The love of God is clothed in the love of the Sacred Heart, and in this consists the glory of the Sacred Heart. For, if the Sacred Heart is the Heart of God, it owns all the glory that belongs to God. Before Our Lord went to suffer for us, He prayed to His Father: "And now glorify Thou Me, O Father . . . with the glory which I had before the world was with Thee" (John 17, 5). What is this glory which He had before the world was? What else but His divine glory.

Divine glory was His garment in the days of eternity before the world was made. Therefore the Sacred Heart is invested and clothed with divine glory, and we look up to this Heart as the Heart of Him who sitteth at the right hand of God in the glory of the Father.

The same Christ who sitteth at the right hand of His Father is also present in the Blessed Sacrament. The same Christ who is adored in heaven because He is God, the same Christ must be adored as God in the Blessed Sacrament. But wheresoever the God-made-Man is present, whether in heaven or on earth, there also is His Heart, and therefore His Heart must be adored as the Heart of God in heaven and on earth. St. Paul writes to the Philippians: "He humbled Himself, becoming obedient unto death, even to the death of the cross. For which cause God also hath exalted Him, and hath given Him a name which is above all names, that in the name of Jesus every knee should bow of those that are in heaven, on earth and under the earth, and that every tongue should confess that the Lord Jesus Christ is in the glory of God the Father" (2, 8-11). He does not say in the name of the Son of God, but in the name of Jesus; that is, in the name of Him who is God and Man at the same time. But this worship is divine worship, and therefore the Sacred Heart must be worshiped as the Heart of God.

Since, then, the Sacred Heart is substantially united to the Word of God, it is evident that the doctrine of the Sacred Heart is an essential part of Catholic doctrine, and we therefore cannot refuse the Sacred Heart divine worship without lapsing into heresy. It also follows that the Catholic Church, in exciting us to devotion to the Sacred Heart, has not invented a devotion which is novel. This devotion is as old as the Church itself. For, the Church took its beginning at the Incarnation, and the Sacred Heart was united to the Word of God at the Incarnation. Therefore, this devotion has always been in the Church from the beginning. The public and solemn veneration as, for instance, on the first Friday of the month, may be called new, but it is new only as to the manner in which the Sacred Heart is to be worshiped. The light of the sun is the same everywhere and always. But when reflected in a prism it appears in various colors. So it is with this devotion. The devotion to, and the doctrine of, the Sacred Heart is always the same. Therefore no one who loves God will find it strange that the Church wants her children to comprehend "what is the breadth and length, and height, and depth of the charity of Christ, that they may be filled unto the fulness of God" (Ephesians 3, 19), all the more so, as the present age is cold and does not appreciate the immense love of God.

Chapter IV

HEART OF JESUS, INFINITE IN MAJESTY

MAJESTY is a quality which produces cold admiration, and does not affect the human heart till the being that possesses that quality proves his title to love by showing that he is loving. Majesty suggests the idea of imposing loftiness and dignity, and dignity is allied to importance. We may admire persons of merit and dignity, but as a rule they are distant; and unless they show that they also have a human heart with a human love, we are not inclined to love them. It is easy to realize the meaning of the majesty and infinite love of God when we see it acted out in every thought, word and deed of Christ, in His dealings with the men and women of his own time and the human hearts of every generation.

The Heart of Jesus is infinite in majesty; that is, its dignity and importance are so great that they transcend our imagination and are beyond the reach of our understanding. For, the Sacred

Heart is the Heart of God. But will this prove an obstacle to our loving the Sacred Heart? Decidedly not. The Sacred Heart is of infinite majesty because it is the Heart of the Man-God Jesus Christ, who made satisfaction to God for our sins. In this satisfaction the Sacred Heart took an active part, because it is the seat of that infinite love which the God-Man Jesus Christ bore for us. Now, the infinite majesty of the Sacred Heart consists in this, and as the Heart of God it urged the Son of God to make infinite satisfaction for us. Therefore, the majesty of the Sacred Heart is its very love, and this infinite love cannot leave us cold, but should win our hearts over to the Sacred Heart, the King and Center of all hearts.

The love of the Sacred Heart was so immense that the Son of God was able to make an adequate satisfaction to His Father. Holy Scripture asserts that the Precious Blood of Christ was the price with which we were bought. It even asserts that it was a great price. A great transaction took place between Christ and His Father. Christ bought heaven for us at the price of His own life and Blood. Yet, He could not have done this if the love of His Heart had not been an infinite love. But because this Heart possessed an infinite dignity and majesty, God the Father forgave us our gilt. "Father, forgive them, for they know not what they do!" (Luke 23, 34).

The infinite majesty of the Sacred Heart appears yet greater by comparing the sacrifices of the Old Testament with the one sacrifice which Christ made. St. Paul says that, though the Jews offered various and many sacrifices every year, they could never take away sin, because there was no proportion between the victim and the purpose for which the victim was killed. But Christ came, and offered Himself to God, and the power of His satisfaction lasts through all times. There is no need for Him to die again; there is no need for Him to satisfy the Divine Justice again; on the contrary, He now sitteth at the right hand of His Father, because He also is God, and inspired His Human Heart with an infinite love, and thus He alone could abolish the sacrifices of the Old Testament and could give us a sacrifice that will never lose its value.

The majesty of the Sacred Heart manifests itself also in its satisfaction, which was superabundant and overflowing. This superabundance has its source in the overflowing love of the Sacred Heart. St. Paul says: "Where sin abounded, grace did more abound" (Romans 5, 20). God permitted man to fall so deeply that His divine love should, by contrast, stand out in bolder relief. Our Lord's agony in the garden reveals to us how dreadful and grievous sin must be. Mortal sin is an insult against God; the sinner turns his back on God, rejects and abandons Him, and rebels against Him. God, who is not wanting in any perfection, is offended. He is the Lord and Master of all things; all creatures must obey Him. But what is man that he dares to offend this great God? He is misery and emptiness and clay, and yet he is not afraid to raise his arm against God. Man employs the gifts of His Maker to offend Him. Sin does harm to God; sin is revolution, is attempted dethronement of God. Now, how many sins have been committed since the first sin? And how many will yet be committed? But "where sin abounded, grace did more abound." It was the love of the Sacred Heart that overcame all obstacles. The Sacred Heart said: I want all men to have life, and have it abundantly. And this superabundance shows itself in this, that not only once were our sins forgiven; they can always be forgiven in the sacrament of Penance. It is easy for us who have sinned to steal quietly into the darkness of a confessional, whisper our sins to a priest who does not know us, and who, once convinced that we are paying the only price that Christ demands—sorrow for our sins—he raises his hand to make the sign of the cross, as he pronounces the words of absolution that wipe out our every sin. But back of that sign of the cross and back of the words of absolution are all the Blood and the horror of the tragedy on Calvary. It was not easy for Christ to purchase this power for His priesthood. It was given and conferred only after the last gasp and the last drop of Blood had been spilt on Calvary. Without the bleeding open Heart of Christ, without Christ on His cross on Calvary, you and I could *shriek* our sins to every man that was ever born, and not one sin would ever be forgiven or forgotten. What a price the Sacred Heart of Christ paid that we may hear from His priesthood the words of strength and consolation: "Go in peace, thy sins are forgiven thee." To make satisfaction for us, Our Lord not only said a prayer, He not only took upon Himself some sufferings and humiliations. His sufferings began in the manger, and came to an end on the cross. The last drop of Blood of the Sacred Heart was shed to redeem us. Our Lord procured for us not only some grace; in seven channels the grace of God flows into our souls, the channels of the holy sacraments. In Holy Communion we even receive the Author of grace, so that, in truth, life and grace were given us in superabundance.

This life and grace are not only superabundant; they are simply infinite, because Christ made an infinite satisfaction, and thus the majesty of the Sacred Heart becomes infinite. The satisfaction of Christ will never be exhausted, the sacraments will never lose their efficacy, divine grace will never be diminished, because Christ's love for us will never cease. The love of the Sacred Heart will never grow cold or weary of us; its love will remain for all eternity. Its love will never change, because it is an unselfish love; it loves us, not because we could ever deserve or merit to be loved, but because it loves us for love's sake, it wants us to be saved and be happy.

The Sacred Heart is also infinite in majesty when we consider the number of hearts to which it brought salvation. Holy Scripture says: "In the multitude of people is the dignity of the King" (Proverbs 14, 28). The dignity of the Sacred Heart surpasses the dignity of the greatest and mightiest earthly king. St. John says: Christ is "the propitiation for our sins, and not for ours only, but also for those of the whole world" (1 John 2, 2). Therefore Our Lord's satisfaction extends to the whole world, and no man is excluded from the love of the Sacred Heart. As Our Lord on the cross became the victim of the sins of all men, so Our Lord continues to offer Himself to Himself, to His Father in the Holy Mass. Hence the kingdom of the Sacred Heart is as big as the world, and all men without exception are its kingdom, and hence all hearts are its subjects. Its dignity therefore transcends the dignity of the greatest and mightiest king.

The majesty of the Sacred Heart, then, consists in this, that its infinite love enabled the Saviour of the world to make an infinite satisfaction for our sins. If the greatness of the love of the Sacred Heart astonishes us and compels us to admire it with the words of St. John: "Behold what manner of charity the Father hath bestowed upon us, that we should be called, and should be, the sons of God (*Ib.* 3, 1), yet, on the other hand, the majesty of this Heart fills us with love because the Evangelist declares: "Having loved His own who were in the world, He loved them unto the end (John 13, 1); that is, not only to the end of His life, but unto excess. Hence the majesty of the Sacred Heart consists in its excessive love for us. Therefore its majesty does not leave us cold, it is not distant, the majesty of its love has brought it very near to us, and we cannot acknowledge it in any better way than by loving this Heart as much as we can. For, though divine, it is also human, and it is the majesty of the sufferings of this Heart that should make it dear to us. For, if an infinite love leaves our hearts cold, could any other demonstration of love induce us to love God?

Chapter V

A TEMPLE or church is a place dedicated to God and destined for His worship. It is a place of prayer, a place that raises our thoughts and hearts heavenwards, a place where we should honor God, and, lastly, a place where we can receive consolation and strength in all the difficulties and hardships of life. The Sacred Heart is a holy temple of God, a living temple, in which the fulness of the Godhead dwells. And since the Sacred Heart is intimately united to the Word of God, it follows that the Sacred Heart fulfils in an eminent degree those duties which we ought to fulfil in the temple of God, the church. The Sacred Heart is, first of all, a prayerful heart. The Sacred Heart always enjoyed the Beatific Vision, and therefore there was no formal necessity for it to pray. But the Sacred Heart loved to pray, it prayed at all times and in all places. Where did the Sacred Heart pray? It prayed in the temple. Jesus Christ

[31]

said to His parents: "How is it that you sought Me? Did you not know that I must be about My Father's business" (Luke 2, 49)? It prayed at table. Before Our Lord fed the people in the desert, He took the loaves and, when He had given thanks, He distributed them to the people (John 6, 11). It prayed in the mountains. When the people wanted to make Him King, He fled into the mountains alone to pray (Matthew 14, 23). The Sacred Heart prayed before the passion. "My Father, if it be possible, let this chalice pass from Me. Nevertheless, not as I will, but as Thou wilt" (*Ib.* 26, 39). The Sacred Heart prayed on the cross: "Father, forgive them, for they know not what they do" (Luke 23, 34).

When did the Sacred Heart pray? On all important occasions. In the desert it prayed forty days and forty nights. Our Lord prayed before He sent out His apostles. He prayed during the day and at night, publicly and privately.

How much and how long did the Sacred Heart pray? It sometimes spent whole days and whole nights in prayer. Our Lord's life was a long prayer. The Sacred Heart acquired holy habits. For, it is said of Our Lord that He went according to His custom to the mount of Olives (*Ib.* 22, 39).

The Sacred Heart is also a heavenly-minded heart. Once Our Lord said to the Jews: "You are from beneath; I am from above. You are of this world; I am not of this world (John 8, 23). The Jews hated and derided Jesus because in their hearts they were a complete contrast to Jesus Christ. They were earthly, and therefore their manner of thinking and acting was earthly. They belonged to the sinful world; Jesus Christ was the only one that did not belong to it. For, what participation should the Sacred Heart have had in this world? It was always pure, holy and heavenly-minded; the dust of worldliness did not soil it. Its feelings and affection were always in perfect harmony with the will of God. The Sacred Heart did not wish to receive anything material from the world. It despised its riches, pomps and pleasures. It was outside the town, in a stable, that the Sacred Heart began to throb; outside the town, before the gates of the city, this Heart ceased to beat. Born in a stable, deprived of everything at death, laid in a grave that was not His own, as such we see Our Lord, the example of perfect contempt of the world. The Sacred Heart demands of us to form ourselves in the same spirit. Christ said to His apostles and also to us: "You are not of this world." If we were of this world, if we were marked with the spirit of this world, the world would recognize us as her own and would not hate and persecute the disciples of Christ. But she does hate and persecute them because Christ has pronounced a terrible woe over her, saying: "Woe to you that are rich; for you have your consolation. Woe to you that are filled; for you shall hunger. Woe to you that now laugh; for you shall mourn and weep" (Luke 6, 24). Thus, Christ condemns and curses the abuse of the things of this world.

Furthermore, the Heart of Jesus is a zealous heart. He could say with the Psalmist: "The zeal of Thy house hath eaten Me up, and the reproaches of them that reproach Thee are fallen upon Me" (Psalm 68, 10). The Son of God wanted to restore the honor of God in this world. Therefore it was necessary that He should be a champion for God's honor and glorification. The Sacred Heart was not only a continual worshiper and adorer of God's majesty. It endeavored to influence men to learn to know, love and serve God.

Indeed, the Sacred Heart was full of zeal for the honor of the Heavenly Father. The Saviour of the world comes to the temple and, behold, He finds therein those that sell oxen and sheep and doves, and money changers. The Sacred Heart is deeply offended by the doings of these people, who, by their haggling and unseemly noise, disturb the pious prayers in the temple. Our Lord makes a scourge of little cords and drives them all out of the temple, the sellers together with their oxen and sheep. He overthrows the tables of the money-changers, the money rolling down the steps of the temple. Why is the Heart of Jesus glowing with a holy anger? Because the house of His Father is being dishonored and being made a house of traffic.

The Sacred Heart was also full of zeal for the salvation of mankind. How deeply does this Heart feel at the misery of mankind. When Our Lord was standing at the grave of His friend Lazarus, He wept. But He wept more bitterly when He approached the Holy City. He wept over the blindness of its people and over the impending destruction of the city. His Heart is excited when He thinks of the possible seduction of so many souls of innocent children, and when He sees the hypocrisy of the Pharisees. "Generation of vipers," He exclaims, and "children of the devil," He calls such men. And when He sees innumerable immortal souls sitting in ignorance, His Heart wants to help them. Hence He says to His apostles: "Do you not say there are yet four months, and then the harvest cometh? Behold, I say to you, lift up your eyes and see the countries; for they are white already to harvest" (John 4, 35). When He sees the world in the abyss of sin, He says: "I have a baptism wherewith I am to be baptized, and how am I straitened until it be accomplished" (Luke 12, 50)?

Suffering is the only gauge of our manhood and of our love. If we would know the depth of our love for another, let us but answer honestly the question, What is our ability and willingness to suffer for that other? If we are able and willing to suffer just occasionally, then our love is an occasional love. If we are willing to suffer only a little, then that "little" is the gauge of our manhood. Christ proved the extent and depth of His love by a willingness and ability to suffer that no mere man could ever have shown.

The Sacred Heart was supremely a suffering Heart; His life was full of labors, travels, troubles and miseries. But all the more so at the end of His life. As rivers flow into the sea and fill it, so all pains streamed into the Sacred Heart and filled it with misery of every kind. Our Lord suffered in His body, in His soul, in his honor and in His good name. All unite in causing Him pain, friends and enemies. From everywhere His enemies bring instruments to torture Him. Of iron they make nails, of thorns they plait a crown, of leather they make scourges, and of wood they make a cross. But His greatest torturers were the Jews, to whom He had done only everything that was good.

The Sacred Heart, then, was a temple of God by its spirit of prayer, by its detachment from the world, by its zeal for the house of God and the salvation of souls, and by its willingness and readiness to suffer. This divine Heart demands imitation of us, and the manner of this imitation is expressed in Holy Scripture thus: May God "give you all a heart to worship Him, and to do His will with a great heart and a willing mind. May He open your heart in His law, and in His commandments, and send you peace" (2 Machabees 1, 3-4). In order to pray as the Sacred Heart prays, we require recollection of our souls and minds, a continual desire to please God and a holy habit to do His will. In order to be heavenly-minded, we should take refuge in the Sacred Heart and should say with the Psalmist: "Conduct me, O Lord, in Thy way, and I will walk in Thy truth. Let my heart rejoice that it may fear Thy name" (Psalm 85, 11). In order to be zealous as the Sacred Heart was, we should love God for His own sake; and in order to be able to suffer with the Sacred Heart, we should avoid murmuring and complaining. For, our love for our King's Heart should spur us on to render ourselves worthy of Him. "For we have not a High Priest who cannot have compassion on our infirmities; but one tempted in all things like as we are, without sin" (Hebrews 4, 15).

Chapter VI

HEART OF JESUS, TABERNACLE OF THE
MOST HIGH

"BEHOLD the tabernacle of God with men, and He will dwell with them. And they shall be His people, and God Himself with them shall be their God" (Apocalypse 21, 3). These words of St. John in the Apocalypse can be applied to the Sacred Heart. In the Old Testament the tabernacle of the covenant had been a temporary dwelling place of God. It had been a token of the union of God with His chosen people at a time when God manifested Himself through prophets. The tabernacle of the covenant had for a time been the religious heart, the center, the sanctuary of a union animated by the spirit of a holy fear of God. But when the same God deigned to speak through His Son, He established a new covenant, a covenant of love. The token of the new union with men is a new tabernacle, the tabernacle of the Sacred Heart. Although the Catholic Church is the visible expression of this new union of God with all men, yet this new union itself took place at the Incarnation, and the Sacred Heart was chosen as the new tabernacle of God, and as such was constituted as the true center and the new sanctuary of the new union of God with men. The Church is the visible expression of the union of love which took place in the Sacred Heart and the most perfect resemblance of that love. Therefore, the true center and heart of the Church, her inmost sanctuary, is the Sacred Heart.

The Sacred Heart, as the tabernacle of the Most High, is, in the first place, the heart and center of the Catholic Church. St. Paul says that the Church is the body of Christ; not His natural body, but His spiritual body. Since the Sacred Heart is the symbol of the love which Christ bestowed on all men by redeeming them, and in particular of the love with which Christ loves the Church, it follows that the love of the Sacred Heart is the very life which flows from Christ into the Church, from the Head into the body. Therefore, this divine love is her life; and, since this life comes to her in the form of love, the Sacred Heart is the true center of the life of the Church. This supernatural love of the Sacred Heart is the supernatural nature of the Church; and, since this supernatural nature of the Church manifests itself chiefly in her dogmas, her moral teachings and her worship, the Sacred Heart becomes a grand text-book of theology.

Take her dogmas. The love of the Sacred Heart leads us to the Owner of this Heart, to Our Lord. We become acquainted with His life, passion and death, resurrection and ascension. We learn that He is God; and, since He is the Second Person of God, we learn of the existence of the Blessed Trinity. The manner of His having become Man introduces to us His Blessed Mother; and the aim of His death tells us that grace is a supernatural gift and therefore not due to us. The Church which He founded is to apply this grace to us, and at the consummation of the world He will come again to judge all men.

Take the moral teachings of the Church. The fundamental aim of the teaching, preaching, instructing and educating of the Church is to make man love God. The ways in which man attains to this love are as manifold as there are

[41]

individuals to be taught to love God. But the aim itself always remains the same: To give men, and to fill their hearts with, the love of God. Those who possess the highest degree of this love are the saints.

The Catholic worship, a love similar to the love of the Sacred Heart, also tends to nothing else. The sacrifice of the Holy Mass and the sacraments are a participation in the immense love of Christ by which we are to be saved.

We see, then, that the Sacred Heart is truly the center of the Church, her heart from which the blood-stream of life, that is, love and grace, flows into the whole body; it is the Sacred Heart that truly unites all the members of the Church into one only man through its love. So much is the Sacred Heart the center of the Church that it wants its love to be incarnated in the hearts of the faithful so that there may be one head, one body, one spirit. Indeed, God has chosen a wonderful tabernacle in the Sacred Heart; God has built a house in which are to dwell those that are of one mind and one spirit. The love of the Master proceeds from His Heart, penetrates the whole body of the Church, and thus becomes the center of those that participate in His love.

Not only is the Sacred Heart the center and gravitating point of the Church; it is also her sanctuary. The tabernacle of the covenant was a place where the Jews temporarily sacrificed, prayed and received graces from God. In the New Testament we have a new sanctuary, a new holy place. St. Paul writes: "Christ loved the Church and delivered Himself up for it, that He might sanctify it, cleansing it by the laver of water in the word of life, that He might present it to Himself a glorious Church, not having spot or wrinkle or any such thing; but that it should be holy and without blemish" (Ephesians 5, 25-27). If the aim of the Church is to sanctify men and to give us God, by what power does she do it? It is by the power of the love of the Sacred Heart. Christ loves the Church as His bride, which means that Christ has given Himself up to the Church, He gives Himself to all her members; in other words, the love of Christ becomes incarnate in the hearts of men. "Dearly beloved," says St. John, "we are now the sons of God; and it hath not yet appeared what we shall be. We know that when He shall appear, we shall be like to Him" (1 John 3, 2). This likeness, according to St. Peter, consists in this, that "we are made partakers of the divine nature" (2 Peter 1-4), and, according to St. Paul, "that we may receive His sanctification" (Hebrews 12, 10). God, then, manifests Himself to us as a Friend to His friend, as a Father to His child, so much so that we may say to Him: Abba, Father. The Church, who wants to show us Jesus, and who wants us to participate in the divine nature, acts through the power of the love of the Sacred Heart. She enters, as it were, into the sanctuary of the Heart of Jesus, and takes its love to give it to us. This she does, in the first place, in the Holy Mass. The Holy Mass is not only a remembrance of the death of Jesus Christ. The same Jesus who offered Himself on the cross offers Himself in the Holy Mass, though in an unbloody manner. The same love that flowed from the Sacred Heart on the cross, also flows from the Sacred Heart on the altar. The Church draws daily from this fountain of love, and pours it out into the hearts of her children, and thereby gives them strength and joy to cope with their great and small crosses.

The Church gives us the love of the Sacred Heart, in the second place, through the holy sacraments, especially through the Holy Eucharist and Confession. In Holy Communion she gives the faithful the Sacred Heart itself, and in Confession she leads them to the merciful love of the Good Samaritan. And when the Church rolls out before our eyes the mysteries of our redemption in the feast days and holy seasons of the year, she has only one object in view: she wants to open ever so many depths of the great mystery of the love of God; she wants to show ever so many new ways of the love and grace of the Sacred Heart. The fountain of this activity of the Church, then, is the Sacred Heart, is her belief that the Eternal Love is present in the tabernacle. And if the Sacred Heart were not her inmost sanctuary, and if she had not the belief in the real presence of Christ in the Blessed Sacrament, she would perhaps be a beautiful but in reality a dead body, a body without a soul.

But, thank God, the Church is a living body which daily receives its life from the love of the Sacred Heart; she is a light which is daily kindled by the light of the love of the Sacred Heart.

A sea of light and love is poured out over the Church; the Sacred Heart is the tabernacle of the Most High, uniting all the members of the Church in love and communicating it to them. Therefore the Church need not fear. "The stream of the river [of the love of the Sacred Heart] maketh the city of God joyful. The Most High hath sanctified His own tabernacle. God is in the widst thereof; it shall not be moved" (Psalm 45, 5-6).

We all know, thank God, and it makes life livable (if not sometimes lovable) what the heart of a friend is. We know what the heart of a father or a brother is; but if we would really understand the Heart of Christ, we must know the heart of a child. As Christ sat that evening at the Last Supper in the midst of twelve ignorant men, He wanted to give us a token worthy of Himself. With the spontaneity of the heart of a child, He gave not only something that He had, but He gave all that He was. He gave Himself, and even God cannot give more than that. The Heart of Christ *is* the heart of a child.

Chapter VII

A CHURCH building is called a house of God. We erect church buildings that truth may find a pulpit, prayer a sanctuary, and love a fire where it can be kindled. The Sacred Heart is truly a house of God, because the fulness of the Godhead dwells in it, and Our Lord assumed this Heart that it might be for us a pulpit where truth is preached, a sanctuary where our prayers are sure to be heard, and a fire where our love is kindled.

The Sacred Heart, then, is a pulpit from which divine truth is announced to the world. Our Lord came down from heaven to tell men that God is love, that He loves them, and that they ought to love Him in return. But truth is something that must be perceived with our intellects through hearing, and therefore must be announced from a place where it can be heard, and that place is the pulpit in the church.

[47]

The Sacred Heart has chosen a pulpit of its own where it preaches to the world, and that pulpit is the Blessed Sacrament. Since the Blessed Sacrament is a memorial of the love of God for us, and since the Sacred Heart is present in the Blessed Sacrament, it is evident that the Blessed Sacrament is the most appropriate pulpit for the great announcement that God is love, and that He loves us. The Blessed Sacrament is the Sacred Heart's perpetual pulpit. The Sacred Heart could have chosen to preach to us at the celebration of the Holy Mass, it could have chosen to be present in one church only, in one province, in one country, in one town. But, no; its pulpit is perpetual and universal. We might almost say that the Sacred Heart has erected a pulpit in nearly every street; for, where there is the Blessed Sacrament, there is the pulpit of the Sacred Heart. The Blessed Sacrament is a pulpit from which the Sacred Heart speaks to all men. Come all to Me, it says. Therefore, if all men are invited, it is clear that the Sacred Heart wants to speak not only to the learned, but also to the unlearned; not only to adults, but also to children; not only to the rich, but also to the poor. This pulpit is not only in beautiful churches; the Sacred Heart erects its pulpit wherever the Blessed Sacrament is carried by the priest. Therefore it may be found in the most miserable houses, and in the poorest chapels and churches, even in dungeons and prisons. At any time men may surround this pulpit; the Sacred Heart is so patient and amiable that it does not interfere with the duties and obligations of its hearers; at all times they may come and listen to the sermon of love.

The Sacred Heart is also a sanctuary for our prayers. Of course, prayer itself is one of the most sublime acts of religion; it is something that we have in common with the angels. We can pray anywhere; we may say our prayers in common or privately. Yet there are places where God is more inclined to listen to our petitions, and there are persons whose prayers are more efficacious than those of others. Our Lord Himself asserts that the prayer said in common is more efficacious than the prayer which is said privately. "Where there are two or three gathered in My name, there am I in the midst of them" (Matthew 18, 20). And Our Lord also says: "Amen, amen, I say to you: If you ask the Father anything in My name, He will give it you" (John 16, 23). We should pray in the name of Jesus, and therefore also in the name of the Sacred Heart, because such a prayer is the most sublime prayer. For then we pray in the name of that Heart in which the Father is well pleased, in the name of that Heart of whose fulness we have all received, in the name of the "High Priest over the house of God" (Hebrews 10, 21), and in the name of the Heart of the Lamb of God. And if this prayer is the most sublime prayer, it is also the most efficacious prayer. For, why should Our Lord have admonished us to pray in His name if He did not wish us to obtain what we ask for? But now He has said it, and it must be true. For He says: "Heaven and earth shall pass away, but My words shall not pass away" (Mark 13, 31). He also confirms His words with a holy oath, saying: "Amen, amen I say to you." Hence there is nothing too great that we could not obtain in the name of the Sacred Heart. For, if we pray with the necessary conditions and dispositions, the blessing of the Sacred Heart will come upon us, and we shall experience a great change in our life.

Lastly, the Sacred Heart is a fire by which our love can be kindled. Our Lord and His apostles strictly command us to love God and our neighbor. Our Lord calls it the greatest commandment, and St. Paul says: If we speak with the tongues of men and of angels and have not charity, we are become as sounding brass or a tinkling cymbal. . . . And if we should distribute all our possessions to the poor, and even die martyrs for the sake of our religion, and have not charity, it will profit us nothing for heaven (1 Corinthians 13, 1-3). For if we do not love God and our neighbor for God's sake, we do not please God, and therefore cannot see Him in heaven. Since man committed sin in paradise, his nature is debilitated, his understanding is darkened, his will weakened, so that he often experiences great difficulty in loving God; that is, in keeping the commandments of God and the Church. Therefore Our Lord said: "I am come to cast fire on the earth, and what will I but that it be kindled" (Luke 12, 49)? The love of the Sacred Heart is that fire by which our love can be kindled. For, the Sacred Heart says to us: "Learn of Me because I am meek and humble." The Sacred Heart possesses a transforming power. If we let ourselves be kindled, it will make us humble, loving God and forgetful of self.

The Sacred Heart is called both a house of God and a gate of heaven. The Sacred Heart is like the ladder which Jacob saw in his sleep, a ladder standing on the earth, with its top reaching heaven (Genesis 20, 12). This ladder signifies the helpful communication in which God is with His faithful servants, especially when they are in distress as Jacob was when he had to flee because of his brother Esau. In a similar way when we say that the Sacred Heart is a gate of heaven, we mean that the Sacred Heart is always ready to help us. It says: Come all to Me. I am in this world, but My message is pointing to heaven. It is the missing link for those who do not believe at all. It leads them to the mystery of the Incarnation, gives them a knowledge of God, who is their Creator, Redeemer and Sanctifier, and brings home to them the duties they have toward God. The Sacred Heart is a physician for men who are ill in their souls. It cures the diseases of religious ignorance, doubt, takes away the fear of men and their sloth. For, the Sacred Heart is not a compromising Heart. For, it says to such men: "I would thou wert cold or hot" (Apocalypse 3, 15). Therefore, those who come in contact with the Sacred Heart will become either cold or hot. It does not tolerate a medium state. For it adds: "Because thou art lukewarm, and neither cold nor hot, I will begin to vomit thee out of My mouth" (*Ib.* 3, 15). Lastly, the Sacred Heart calls those who are healthy and strong; that is, those who faithfully practice their religion. To them the Sacred Heart wants to be a guiding Friend. St. Paul admonishes them saying: "He that thinketh himself to stand, let him take heed lest he fall" (1 Corinthians 10, 12). And St. John gives this advice: "He that is just, let him be justified still; and he that is holy, let him be sanctified still" (Apocalypse 22, 11).

When we remember what heavenly treasures are stored up in the Sacred Heart, we should gladly enter into this house of God where we find the pulpit of truth, the sanctuary of prayer and the fire of love. Once we are sheltered in this house, it will at the same time become for us a gate of heaven. For, whether we are luke-warm or careless, ignorant or wavering, cold or hot—"let us go with confidence to the throne of grace [of the Sacred Heart] that we may obtain mercy and find grace in seasonable aid" (Hebrews 4, 16).

Chapter VIII

HEART OF JESUS, BURNING FURNACE
OF CHARITY

THE Sacred Heart of Jesus is compared to a
furnace. A furnace is an inclosed structure
in which is kept up a strong fire for the purpose
of melting metals. In the Sacred Heart there is
kept up the fire of divine love for the purpose of
melting human hearts and moving them to return the love of the Sacred Heart. The love of
God is blazing in the Sacred Heart with seven
flames.

The first flame is the flame of forgiving love.
The Sacred Heart prayed for its murderers:
"Father, forgive them, for they know not what
they do" (Luke 23, 34). Our Lord did not pray
on His own behalf, for He was without sin. But
since He came to save the lost sheep, He also
prayed for His murderers, and for all His
enemies. From this it follows that we may have
the greatest confidence that God will forgive
us our sins if we pray in the name of Jesus. But

the Our Father teaches us that we must first forgive others before we can expect God to forgive us our own sins. Therefore, forgiving love is the first condition of a true devotion to the Sacred Heart. For the Sacred Heart has given us a new commandment, that we should love not only our friends, but also our enemies. For, Our Lord says: "I say to you, Love your enemies, do good to them that hate you, and pray for them that persecute and calumniate you" (Matthew 5, 44). The Sacred Heart practiced this commandment so heroically that we cannot be its disciples if we cannot bring ourselves to forgive all our enemies from the bottom of our hearts. But if we do so, the Sacred Heart will bless us, it will forgive us our own trespasses, it will reward us and, above all, it will give us that peace which the world cannot give us.

The love of the Sacred Heart, in the second place, is a love of infinite mercy. The good thief on the cross said to Jesus: "Lord, remember me when Thou shalt come into Thy kingdom. And Jesus said to him: Amen, I say to thee, this day thou shalt be with Me in paradise" (Luke 23, 42-43). The good thief had been a bad man, a thief and robber who had maybe taken many an innocent life. He saw Jesus hanging on the cross, and at once realized that Jesus had done no wrong. For, he said to his fellow-accomplice: "We receive the due rewards for our deeds, but this man hath done no evil" (*Ib.* 23, 41). Hence he said to Jesus: "Lord, remember me when Thou shalt come into Thy kingdom." Our Lord did not reject the petition of this thief. His task had always been to look for lost sheep. He had found them everywhere, at the well of Jacob as well as in the custom house of Capharnaum, on the high road to Damascus as well as in the house of Simon the leper. Now He was finding a lost sheep hanging on a cross. The Sacred Heart in its infinite love could not abandon this sheep, and so the good thief obtained the forgiveness of his sins; he was sorry for his sins, and therefore needed not despair. On the contrary, since his penance was so great, he merited to be received into heaven straightway. The same love and pity for poor sinners we should be animated with. However sinful a man may be, we have no right to despise him; for, as long as he lives here below, he might do penance. If

God suffers the cockle to grow together with the wheat, we may not tear it up. For, we are told not to judge, that we may not be judged. If God so loved the world as to give His only-begotten Son, we should at least pray for poor sinners and help them to return to God.

The love of the Sacred Heart is also a love of infinite care. "When Jesus had seen His Mother, and the disciple standing whom He loved, He said to His Mother: Woman, behold thy son. After that, He said to the disciple: Behold thy Mother" (John 19, 26-27). The Sacred Heart respected the fourth commandment even on the cross. Jesus Christ is the Creator of heaven and earth, He is the ruler of the world, He is the supreme Judge of all men, and yet He was subject to Mary and Joseph. Even when He was hanging on the cross, He did not forget to look after His Mother. He did not forget the love and care His parents had bestowed upon Him. His Heart had always been grateful to them. Now His gratitude shows itself in deed. He confides His Mother to the care of St. John. From the Sacred Heart, we should learn how to be obedient. Children should learn to be obedient to their parents, wives to their husbands, citizens to the civil authorities, and Catholics to the Pope, bishops and priests. It is especially to the Catholic Church that we owe obedience and love. For, she is the supreme authority in the world, she is our infallible guide in matters of faith and morals, she is an authority of which Christ has said: "He that heareth you, heareth Me; and he that despiseth you, despiseth Me."

Furthermore, the love of the Sacred Heart was a love full of zeal for souls. St. John relates: "Afterwards Jesus, knowing that all things were accomplished that the Scripture might be fulfilled, said: I thirst" (*Ib*. 19, 28). Our Lord's physical thirst was great, but greater was His thirst for souls. To gain souls, to save them, to deliver them from the power of Satan, to make them happy and to lead them to heaven, this, and this alone was the object of His coming down from heaven. Our Lord only lived for souls, because, having loved them, He loved them unto the end. All the prayers He said, all the journeys He undertook, all the cares He had and all the sufferings He underwent were so many manifestations of His burning thirst for souls. Also in this point we should imitate the Sacred Heart. We can help Our Lord to save souls by being apostles ourselves in our families, at our work, in society and by supporting ecclesiastical associations by prayer and alms.

The love of the Sacred Heart was no less a love full of confidence in God. "About the ninth hour Jesus cried with a loud voice: My God, My God, why hast Thou forsaken me?" (Matthew 27, 46). In these words Our Lord expressed all the pain of His Heart forsaken by God. The Sacred Heart wanted to suffer this abandonment to atone for our sins. But Our Lord knew that God would not abandon Him forever, but that His Heart would be filled with happiness when the work of redemption was accomplished. The Sacred Heart made suffering venerable. He did not refuse to drink the chalice. He thereby gave us an example how to bear our sufferings. We should unite our sufferings with His. He also experienced and felt pain and sorrow, but He also prayed: Not Mine, but Thy will be done. He showed us the greatness of the reward if we suffer patiently. Our sufferings lead us to the glory of heaven, as Our Lord said to the disciples going to Emmaus: "Ought not Christ to have suffered these things and so to enter into His glory?" (Luke 24, 26).

The love of the Sacred Heart was also a love of perseverance. St. John says: "Jesus, therefore, when He had taken the vinegar, said: It is consummated" (John 19, 30). The Sacred Heart loved men unto the death of the cross, and thus saved us. We also must persevere; because if we do not, we cannot be crowned. We belong to God, we come from Him and He commands us to strive after perfection in order that we may be fit to see God in heaven. We can persevere, because God's grace is powerful enough to make us triumph over the enemies of salvation. And since we have that power, it needs only a firm resolution of our will to persevere, and to make use of vigilance and prayer that we may not be overcome.

Lastly, the love of the Sacred Heart was a love of piety. "And Jesus, crying with a loud voice, said: Father, into Thy hands I commend My spirit" (Luke 23, 46). The Sacred Heart no longer looked for human consolation. It wanted to be with the heavenly Father. How many people even in their last hour think only of earthly things, but what can they profit them? What a hapiness for us to be able to die in the love of the Sacred Heart! If we die in this love, earthly things will no longer mean anything to us, our closing eyes will behold God, who has come to take us into heaven, where there will be no sufferings any more, where an immense happiness will be our share, a happiness which will last forever.

Chapter IX

HEART OF JESUS, ABODE OF JUSTICE
AND LOVE

THE love of the Sacred Heart reveals to us not only the goodness of God, but also His justice. On the cross love and justice ruled together; nay, love was subservient to justice. For, the Son of God became Man to make satisfaction by His passion and death for the misdeeds of mankind. Since God is holy and must punish sin, divine justice had to take its course in the manner it pleased God. Whatever men might do to appease the divine wrath, they could never make adequate satisfaction. And adequate satisfaction had to be made, as the history of the Redemption shows. True, "God so loved the world as to give His only-begotten Son" (John 3, 16). But, notwithstanding the fact that He loved the world so immensely that He sent His only Son to make satisfaction for us and in our stead, yet His very love was prompted by justice. For, seeing that we could not make adequate satisfaction, He had pity on us and, in demanding of His Son to make an adequate satisfaction, He at the same time showed us the greatness of His love by giving us His Son.

Since Our Lord's first aim was to make satisfaction and appease the divine wrath and justice, it is evident that His Heart had a share in that satisfaction. St. Paul says: "God hath proposed Christ Jesus to be a propitiation, through faith in His Blood to the showing of His justice, for the remission of former sins, through the forbearance of God, for the showing of His justice in this time" (Romans 3, 25-26). If God wanted to reveal not only His love but also His justice in Jesus Christ, the Sacred Heart also is not only a revelation of God's love, but also of His justice. In other words, the Sacred Heart also reveals and demonstrates the holiness of God, who did not want to let sin go unpunished.

If we wish to know how holy God is and how much He hates sin, we need only ask ourselves how much the Sacred Heart loves us; and if we wish to know how much the Sacred Heart loves us, we need only remember how much Our Lord suffered for us. Hence, the Sacred Heart reveals to us the justice of God by reminding us of the sufferings Our Lord underwent for us. These sufferings are an eloquent expression of the feelings of justice that were in the Sacred Heart, which the Church calls an abode of justice and love.

The Sacred Heart is the interpretation of God's justice. It loves us so much because it was at a high price that Our Lord had to buy us. But the price was so very high because God was not content with some satisfaction, but with a proportionate one. The love of the Sacred Heart is the measure of the divine justice. If Jesus Christ had not come into this world; if He had not borne our infirmities and carried our sorrows; if He had not been wounded for our iniquities and bruised for our sins; if we had not been healed by His bruises—what should we know of the malice of sin and of the displeasure it causes God? And if the Sacred Heart did not so forcibly remind us of the Only-begotten of the Father who came down from heaven, led a life of misery and toil and was nailed to a cross for our sins, what should we know of the justice of God?

The Sacred Heart is the greatest proof that God is infinitely just. It was not an angel who came down to redeem us, nor a holy prophet who died for us; God Himself deigned to show us how greatly He had been offended by us. The Deluge was certainly a great manifestation of God's hatred of sin; so was also the fire and brimstone that rained over the sinful cities of Sodom and Gomorrha. But what are these punishments compared to the spectacle of Golgotha? What are they compared to that excess of love which so tragically reveals the divine justice? The king in the gospel remitted his servant the payment of the huge sum of ten thousand talents. But what are ten thousand talents compared to the debt we had contracted? The Sacred Heart tells us that we owe it to Christ that we are delivered from the bonds of sin and that we enjoy the liberty of the children of God; we owe it to Our Lord that we may enter into heaven. Christ bought us, saved us, enriched us. The greatness of His love demonstrates the greatness of God's justice. Even more. One drop of His Precious Blood would have been sufficient to save us. But, no; to show us the greatness of the divine justice, He died the most cruel, the most infamous, the most disgraceful death, the death on a cross, the death of a slave, the death of a criminal.

If we wish to be true followers of the Sacred Heart, we should learn from it to know and detest the malice of sin. St. Peter writes: "Christ suffered for us, leaving you an example that you should follow His steps. Who did no sin, neither was guile found in His mouth. Who His own self bore our sins in His own body on the tree that we, being dead to sin, should live to justice" (1 Peter 2, 21-22, 24). This is the admonition of the first Pope. For, what man would like to offend the Sacred Heart, the abode of justice and love, if he seriously thinks upon the sufferings which His Lord and Master, Friend and Benefactor, sustained for His sins? Christ did not refuse to die when there was question of destroying sin. This shows that sin was, in His eyes, a far greater evil than His death on the cross. But when we do not live to justice but commit sin, "we crucify again the Son of God to ourselves, and make Him a mockery," as the Apostle says (Hebrews 6, 6). We renew His sufferings, we scourge Him, crown Him with thorns, and nail Him to the cross. Christ must detest our sins, because He suffered for them. St. Paul says that the Jews would never have crucified Him if they had known Him as the King of Glory (1 Corinthians 2, 8). But we know who Our Lord is, we know that He has the words of eternal life, we believe that He is the Way, the Truth and the Life, and yet we dare to offend Him. We cannot excuse ourselves, saying: God is good, He will not mind. Did Jesus Christ not say: "If in the green wood they do these things, what shall be done in the dry?" (Luke 23, 31).

God did not spare His only Son: He died on Mount Calvary under the strokes of divine justice. He died although He was sinless, only because He wanted to make vicarious satisfaction for us. Now, if even the innocent died for sins He never committed, what punishment will await him who does not cease renewing the pains and sufferings of Christ? If God did not spare His Son, will He spare a Catholic who continues to offend Him?

Let us never forget this truth: Sin is not a

trifling thing, God punishes it terribly. He who meditates seriously on the pains of the God-Man Jesus Christ hanging on the cross, to him the existence of hell cannot be a mere imagination. If he loves the Sacred Heart, he will learn of it how to live to justice. For, it is through the love of the Sacred Heart that he is healed from the wounds of his sins.

We must never forget how Christ and the world look upon sin. The world thrown a glamor around sin to make its every aspect attractive. The world loves sin, but it despises the sinner who has been caught. Christ hates sin, tries constantly to make us realize that it is all a horrible mistake and, at the same time, we see the intensity of His love for the sinner.

Chapter X

HEART OF JESUS, FULL OF KINDNESS
AND LOVE

"CHARITY is kind," says St. Paul (1 Corinthian 13, 4). We know that the Sacred Heart is a revelation of the love of God for man. But love is manifold in its manifestation. The Sacred Heart is full of goodness and love. This means that its love is kindness, kindness in such a degree that the Sacred Heart is the kindest of all hearts.

A kind heart is disposed to do good to others and to make them happy. Could we imagine a kinder heart, a heart more disposed to do good to others and to make them happy than the Heart of the God-Man Jesus Christ? Sacred History has left us convincing proofs of the kindness of the Sacred Heart. It shows us the Sacred Heart as the noble Heart of the greatest and sincerest Friend of the people. The Evangelist St. Matthew depicts a touching scene of the feeding of the 5,000 people in the desert.

Jesus and the people are in a desert place, far away from the noise of the busy world. The sun is just setting, the dark shadows of the on-coming night are slowly creeping over the waters of the sea; we behold thousands of people sitting on the grass—men, women and children—who, attracted by the charm of the Preacher, have followed Him and now have nothing to eat. Their eyes are fixed with attention and expectation on the great Miracle-worker. What is He going to do for them in this desert place? The disciples are alarmed and suggest sending them away. In the midst of the people sits Jesus, the true Householder who gives his family their measure of wheat in due season (Luke 12, 42). The Friend of the people says: I have compassion on the multitude, they need not go away. His Heart loves these people, they are in need, they must be helped; for the Sacred Heart is a kind Heart, the kindest of all. He says to His apostles: Bring to Me the loaves and the fishes. He blesses them and, like stewards at the Householder's command, the apostles go round serving the bread and the fish. All the people ate and had their fill; for the Sacred Heart was kind to them, the need of the people manifested the

Sacred Heart as a kind Heart. So great was its kindness that the kind act itself was a great miracle.

Since Our Lord came to seek that which was lost, He described His task to the Pharisees in these words: "They that are in health need not a physician, but they that are ill" (Matthew 9, 12). The Sacred Heart was kind to the sick. The Evangelist St. John unrolls before our eyes a picture of the good Heart of the heavenly Physician. He takes us to Jerusalem to a pond called the sheep-pond. This pond was surrounded by porches wherein lay many sick people, blind and lame and withered. The water of the pond possessed healing powers. He that first went into the water after its motion was made whole. Among the sick people we find a man who has been ill thirty-eight years. Our Lord, moved by the helpless and miserable state of the man, begins a conversation with him, and thus He learns that the man has been ill for a long time. The Sacred Heart is touched by the tale of the sick man. It wants to be kind to him, and therefore Our Lord asks him: "Wilt thou be made whole?" Jesus wants to raise in the man hope of recovery and faith in Himself. How fervently the sick man wants to recover from his illness he indicates in the answer he gives to Jesus: "Sir, I have no man when the water is troubled to put me into the pond. For whilst I am coming, another goeth down before me." One word of the Sacred Heart makes the sick man whole: "Arise, take up thy bed and walk." The man was made whole, he took up his bed and walked. But the task of the Sacred Heart was not yet finished. Our Lord is a heavenly physician who taketh away the sins of the world. Many sicknesses were the result of the sinful life of those healed. Afterwards Our Lord found the same man in the temple and said to him: "Behold, thou hast been made whole; sin no more lest some worse thing happen to thee." The Sacred Heart had read the soul of the man. Our Lord admonishes him with strict words not to sin again, not only lest his former sickness might become worse, but also lest through his repeated sins he might fall into the hands of the strict Judge. The good Heart of the heavenly Physician had given back to the sick man the welfare of both his body and soul.

If the Sacred Heart was kind in its love to all men, it was all the more so in its love of its friends. The Sacred Heart is the Heart of the most loving and most powerful of friends. The history of the raising of Lazarus will illustrate this truth. That Our Lord and Lazarus were friends is evident from the message which the sisters of Lazarus, Mary and Martha, sent to Jesus. They simply said: "Lord, behold, he whom Thou lovest is sick." They do not say: "Come and heal him." It is a foregone conclusion to them that the Friend will come to help His friend. But the Friend's Heart *seems* to be apathetic. For, His reply is a mysterious one: "This sickness is not unto death, but for the glory of God, that the Son of God may be glorified by it." And although Lazarus was dangerously ill, He did not go to see Him. When he had died, Jesus said to His apostles: "Lazarus, our friend, sleepeth; but I go that I may wake him out of sleep. It was not apathy, but the will of God, who wanted to glorify Jesus, that He did not go to see Lazarus. When Jesus arrived at Bethania, Lazarus had been dead for days already. Martha and Mary met Him. He sees Mary weeping and the Jews that are with her. He groans in spirit, troubles Himself and says: "Where have you laid him? They say to Him: Lord, come and see." And Jesus weeps. He weeps over the dead friend. He sheds tears elicited from an affectionate love for the dead friend, and sincere sympathy with the dead friend's sorrowful sisters. How lovely are these tears, the tears of the Sacred Heart. Even the Jews said: "Behold how He loved Him." The Saviour has not arrived at the friend's grave. Again He is perturbed: He orders the stone in front of the grave to be taken away. Before the open grave now stands Jesus. He raises His eyes in prayer to His Father, and then He cries into the grave with a loud voice: "Lazarus, come forth." His almighty words break the power of death, Lazarus appears in the opening of the grave, still bound feet and hands with winding bands, and his face wound about with a napkin. Jesus says to his sisters: "Loose him and let him go." The Evangelist says nothing about the astonishment of those that saw the miracle, nothing about the joy of the sisters of Lazarus. But we know: The Saviour's Heart is the Heart

[75]

of the most loving and most powerful of friends.

But what shall we say of the kindness of the Sacred Heart toward sinners? How merciful was not the Sacred Heart toward Mary Magdalen. St. Luke says she was a sinner in the city (7, 37). We know what sins are meant. The grace of conversion had to accomplish a great work in her soul. Like some sick person, she goes into the house of Simon the Pharisee, where she knows Jesus to be present. She begins to wash His feet with her tears and wipes them with the hair of her head and anoints them with ointment. Christ, the Searcher of hearts, knows that her contrition has washed away her many sins. Simon the Pharisee despised her; not so the Saviour of souls. He was merciful because He knew the love of her heart was very great. He even defended her to the Pharisee: "Many sins are forgiven her because she hath loved much." Then He said to her: "Thy sins are forgiven thee," and dismissed her as a saint; for she became one of the most fervent disciples of Christ.

How true it is that Our Lord came to call the sick, and not those that are healthy. What He did to Mary Magdalen He did to many. And what He did to many, He will do to all that seek Him as Mary Magdalen sought Him. For, in His kindness He does not break the bruised reed, nor extinguish smoking flax (Matthew 12, 20). It is a great consolation for us to know that the Heart of hearts lives in the Blessed Sacrament. Here we find the same Saviour, with the same noble, sympathetic powerful, kind and merciful Heart. The people to whom He was so kind believed and confided in Him, and thus experienced His kindness in such a miraculous way. The same kind Heart is near us; let us open our hearts to this great Heart with a child-like confidence and faith, and we also shall experience how sweet and kind the Sacred Heart is. We should revert occasionally to the simple definition of St. Thomas when he is speaking of love. Love, he tells us, is nothing more than wishing well to the one that you love, joined with the desire to share all your gifts and possessions with the one that you love. How clearly the entire life of Christ brings this out for us.

Chapter XI

HEART OF JESUS, ABYSS OF ALL VIRTUES

THE aim of Catholic education is to bring up men of perfect love, men who have stripped their hearts of all selfishness and dilated them into a holy temple of God, decorated with all Christian virtues. We are to express the virtues of Christ in our lives "until we all meet into the unity of faith, and of the knowledge of God, unto a perfect man, unto the measure of the age of the fulness of Christ" (Ephesians 4, 13). But as even in earthly things there is a gulf between ideal and reality, there must of necessity be an abyss, a gulf where and when divine and human things meet. We are to express in our lives supernatural virtues, holy habits, which we could not so much as think of if God did not lend us His help. The divine element combines itself with the human element, and the consequence is that the divine element cannot display itself in an infinite way and measure because man is a finite being.

The Heart of Jesus is held up to us a pattern of all virtues. And certainly Our Lord practiced all virtues; there was no sin in Him; He loved God and men. He was so humble and meek that He could say to us: "Learn of Me, because I am meek and humble of Heart." He was obedient unto death; He had the greatest patience with His disciples and never broke down under persecutions and hardships.

But the Sacred Heart is an abyss of all virtues; there is a gulf between our virtues and His virtues, and this abyss consists in this: that He practiced all virtues in a measure simply transcending all human measure. This gulf is very conspicuous when we consider that there was the most perfect harmony and proportion between Our Lord's virtues so that one virtue was not detrimental to the other. With us imperfect men the case is quite different. Where do we find a person who is just as humble as he is meek, and just as patient as he is generous, and so forth; in other words, we do not find anyone who possesses all virtues, and in exactly the same degree.

This truth is strikingly reflected by the various

types of saints. Compare the hermit with the saint of industrial centers; the great missionary with the holy patron of blind and crippled people; the cultured and learned saint with the saint walking about in sackcloth—and you will find that each saint became holy through the practice of a particular virtue which was stronger in him than his other virtues and which regulated them. But you will not find a saint who possessed every other saint's particular virtue in the same degree. The reason for this truth is that, though we have to imitate the Sacred Heart as the pattern of all virtues, we are not able to absorb all the rays of holiness that proceed from Christ, the Light of the world, and to transform them into spiritual energy. We, so to say, practice one virtue at the expense of another. Our particular virtue is always in danger of becoming our particular weakness. A meek man may easily become a weak man, a zealous man a hard man, and so forth. Hence the author of the *Following of Christ* is right in saying that in this life perfection is accompanied by imperfection.

Only Our Lord proves an exception to this

rule; for, in Christ there is light without shadow. He possessed all virtues, and each virtue in the same degree. In the Sacred Heart we find virtues which to our human eyes seem incompatible with each other. Christ possessed childlike simplicity, and yet He was at the same time wonderfully prudent. He was as tender as a mother and meek as a lamb, but He also had the strong will of a hero. He was so humble that He could point to His humility as our example; and yet His dignity was so overwhelming that the people had an impression of Him as a man who speaks with power. He was full of zeal, so much so that sometimes He had no time to eat; and yet He spent whole nights in prayer with God. His love for souls was immense, patient, kind and merciful, but at the same time His sense of justice was very grave. He was just, but never hard; He could be indignant, and yet was never angry. All the holiness of the saints, all the virtues that can be thought of, are contained in the Sacred Heart. These virtues are the spirit of Christ, the spirit of the Sacred Heart. As light when reflected in a prism appears in the manifold colors of the rainbow, so the spirit of Christ when absorbed by His followers becomes humility in the one, obedience in another, prudence in a third; and, although divided, this spirit is always one and the same, because the Sacred Heart is the fountain and divine original of all virtues, a fountain from which all virtues flow and an original which can be imitated, but not equalled. We stand before an abyss which we cannot cross.

When standing at the edge of an abyss we often experience a sensation of giddiness, and we quickly draw back with a jerk. The very heroism of the virtues of the saints makes us sometimes afraid and down-hearted. No doubt, their great labors, struggles and works of penance were necessary to make them holy. Yet a certain appearance of violence and excess makes us look upon them as superhuman and keeps us away from them. Here, again, the Sacred Heart is an abyss of all virtues, an abyss that does not make us dizzy or down-hearted. The Sacred Heart wants to attract all hearts, but it could hardly succeed if the example of its virtues were rigid and cold. On reading the gospel, we gain the conviction that its holiness

is amiable and imitable. Christ possessed the
ideal human nature. His nature was so beautiful that once He attracted the hearts of some
Greeks, who said to Philip: "Sir, we would see
Jesus" (John 12, 21). Ever since He came on
earth, He has attracted millions of men. For
He says: "Come to Me, all you that labor and
are burdened, and I will refresh you. Take up
My yoke upon you, and learn of Me because I
am meek and humble of Heart. And you shall
find rest to your souls. For My yoke is sweet,
and My burden light" (Matthew 11, 28-30).
Jesus Christ calls those that labor and are burdened, those that are laden with sin and pressed
down by the burden of this life. He sees them
go along, walking under a heavy yoke, the yoke
of sin, the yoke of the world and the yoke of
Satan. Our Lord stands by the roadside. They
see Him in His holiness and sanctity, but they
are afraid to follow Him; so bent are they under
their yoke that they do not even think of throw-
ing it off. Therefore Christ calls them. His
voice is sweet, His Heart betrays emotion.
"Come to Me," He cries out; "come to Me, all
you that are burdened, and I will refresh you.

Try My yoke, I am the Saviour of souls; come into My school, listen to Me, I want to be your teacher, and if you want to learn of Me, you will be refreshed." What is the refreshment He will give them? He says: "Learn of Me: Become meek, learn to bear injuries with a patient heart." He says: "Become humble, learn to serve the least of your brethren."

Meekness and humility are the foundations of rejuvenescence of the soul. True, also Our Lord lays a yoke on our shoulders. But it does not hurt; it is sweet. Also, Our Lord gives us a burden to carry, but this burden does not press us down; it is light. To cling to the Saviour of the world, to be absorbed in the love of His Sacred Heart, this is the yoke, and this is the burden of the Sacred Heart. Those that are men of good will cannot notice Our Lord without loving Him, and they cannot love Him without becoming similar to Him. And, seeing and loving Him, we shall forget that we stand at the edge of an abyss; and, attracted by His goodness, we shall joyfully precipitate ourselves into the abyss of all virtues. And though this abyss is unfathomable, and though we shall never be able to absorb the spirit of Christ in its infinity, yet we shall find rest to our souls if we allow ourselves to be swallowed up by the abyss of the love of the Sacred Heart, so that we can say with St. Paul: "And I live, now not I; but Christ liveth in me" (Galatians 2, 20).

How true it is, as Father Meschler, S.J., says, "It is easier to go directly to Christ in order to be good, than to try to get to Christ by being good." This could not be true if the Heart of Christ was not all that we know it to be.

Chapter XII

HEART OF JESUS, MOST WORTHY
OF ALL PRAISE

Praise is a commendation bestowed on a person. We recommend that person to someone else as worthy of his confidence, notice or kindness. When praising God, this commendation assumes the form of joyful homage or gratitude. For, God is the Supreme Good, Goodness itself; and hence He is not only worthy of our confidence and notice, but we are bound to recognize and adore Him as such because He is our Lord and Master. Therefore, our praise of God quite naturally turns into gratitude toward Him. The Church recommends to us the Sacred Heart as most worthy of all praise. She presents to us the Sacred Heart as most worthy of our confidence and notice; and since this Heart is also divine, as most worthy of our gratitude.

That which makes the Sacred Heart most worthy of all praise is its infinite love. We should never forget that the Sacred Heart is a revelation of God's love. It brought us the love of God. St. Paul says: "Now there remain faith, hope and charity, these three; but the greatest of these is charity" (1 Corinthians 13, 3). The love of God is the greatest, the most precious and the most essential virtue; and since the Sacred Heart brought us this virtue, it deserves all our praise.

A meditation on the greatness of this gift will reflect the greatness of praise and gratitude that is due to the Sacred Heart. The love of God is greater than all other virtues so far as its nature is concerned. For, love tends to union with God, the Supreme Good. Faith makes us know of the existence of the Supreme Good. Hope makes us desire it, but love unites us to it. By loving the Supreme Good we want to be one with it. Love is precisely the bond that unites the soul to God. "If any one love Me," says Our Lord, "he will keep My word, and My Father will love Him, and We will come to him, and will make Our abode with him" (John 14, 23). From these words it follows that by love we possess the Supreme Good, we enjoy God. As children lovingly cling to father or mother, we cling to God, whose supernatural children we have become; and as children delight in their parents, so we delight in the greatness and perfections of God, our supernatural Father. By love we acquire the right to say to God: Abba, Father. Jesus Christ taught us to address God with the sweet name of Father. He said to us: Address My Father as your Father. Hence we say to God: Our Father, Father of your children, heavenly Father of your supernatural children. All this is effected by love; love brings us near to God, love links us up with God, love is the center of our religion. Christianity without love is hypocrisy and lip service. "I am come to cast fire on the earth," says Our Lord, "and what will I but that it be kindled" (Luke 12, 48-49). Love, then, is a fire. But where there is a fire, something is burning. Where there is a fire, there also is warmth and light. If I enter into a warm room, I know there must be a fire though I may not see it. We cannot see the love of God that is poured forth in our hearts; if we are fervent, if we do good works, we know that the fire of love is kindled in our hearts. But if we do not do good works, if we are indifferent to God, if we do not love our neighbor, if we are careless as to our religious duties, we may be sure that the fire of the love of God is burning low. There is one infallible sign by which we may ascertain if we have the love of God or not. If we are in a state of sanctifying grace, we possess the love of God. Love is the surest sign that we are children of God. He who does not regard his neighbor as his brother is not a child of God. He who hates and lives at enmity with his neighbor is not a child of God. He who transgresses a commandment of God in an important matter is not a child of God. So important is the love of God that Our Lord says to us: "Let your light shine before men that they may see your good works and glorify your Father, who is in heaven" (Matthew 5, 16). Our love of God is to be a proof of the existence of God. For, he who loves God thereby shows that there is a God whom He loves. The non-Catholics are to conclude from our works of love that there is a God of love.

The love of God also excels the other virtues in force and efficacy. St. Paul writes: "Love is the fulfilling of the law" (Romans 13, 1), which means that love includes all the other duties we have to fulfil, love requires the existence of all other virtues, love collects all the flowers of virtues and unites them into a beautiful wreath, and this wreath is only pleasing to God if it is scented with the love of God. When we view the words of St. Paul "Love is the fulfilling of the law" in the light of practical Christianity, we must say that a Catholic who loves God will be a faithful, pure, charitable, kind and obedient Catholic, a Catholic who loves to pray and give alms, a Catholic who loves his Church and is zealous in the fulfillment of the duties of his state. So great is the efficacy of the love of God that it enables man to make the greatest sacrifices for his religion. Witness the holy martyrs, who laid down their lives for their faith; witness the religious people who sacrifice fortune, family and even their own will to love God perfectly. Witness all those good Catholics who in obedience to God and the Church daily fulfil the duties of their state with a great joy of heart and peace of mind.

The love of God is also greater than the other virtues when considered in its aim. The object

of every virtue is to make us like to God. But
St. Paul says: "The end of the precept is charity"
(1 Timothy 1, 5). Two truths follow from these
words. The one is: Love makes us like to God
to a greater extent than any other virtue. All
the other virtues, such as, obedience, temperance,
patience, etc., are to prepare the way for the
coming of the queen. Love is the end and aim
of our life. For we are on earth to do the will
of God. But the will of God is love. All that
Our Lord said and did, all the mysteries of our
religion, all these things tend to excite us to love
God. All the other virtues, then, are the servants of love, which is the queen, and they are
virtues only if and in so far as they tend to and
are subordinate to love, their crown and perfection. But there is yet another truth that follows
from the assertion that love is the end of every
precept. Love is greater in duration than all the
other virtues. St. Paul says: "And now remain
faith, hope, charity; these three." He means to
say that our present life turns round and centers in the exercise of these three great virtues.
Faith remains as long as we do not see God face
to face. But when we begin to see Him face to

face, faith will cease to exist. Hope remains as long as we have to wait for the promises of God to be fulfilled. But when we begin to possess God in heaven, hope will be changed into possession. But charity never falleth away, love will remain for all eternity. For it will be our crown, our perfection, our joy, our bliss. But what we are without this love, the same St. Paul clearly points out when he says that we are nothing, absolutely nothing without love. We may be the greatest lights, the holiest prophets and the most charitable men—if we have not the love of God, we are nothing.

From this meditation, then, it follows, on the one hand, that the love of God is the greatest gift; and, on the other, that it is necessary for us to have this gift. The conclusion is at hand. The Sacred Heart is worthy of all praise, worthy of our gratitude, because it gave us the most precious treasure of divine love. And this praise ought to be the more fervent because the Sacred Heart gave us this gift though we did not even ask for it. The Sacred Heart made the first step, but we must make the second. Holy Scripture tells us that God in the company of two angels appeared to Abraham. When he saw them, he ran from the door of his tent to meet them. This is what is meant by making the second step. The Sacred Heart daily passes by the tent of our soul. And daily we should run to meet this sweetest of hearts, and say to it: "Sacred Heart, if I have found favor in Thy sight, pass not away from Thy servant. Enter into my house, be my sweet Guest, and make Thyself at home in the house of my soul forever."

Chapter XIII

HEART OF JESUS, KING AND CENTER
OF ALL HEARTS

THE Jews led Our Lord to Pilate, who asked Him: "Art Thou a king, then? Jesus answered: Thou sayest that I am a king" (John 18, 37). A king is a man invested with supreme authority over a nation and is to look after the temporal welfare of his people. A king's subjects owe him obedience; but not every king is obeyed because his people love him. Most people obey because they are compelled by laws to obey. As in other respects, so also in this, Our Lord's kingdom is not of this world. Our Lord imposes upon His subjects obedience, but He condemns the obedience of slaves. He is not only a King ruling over the hearts of men; He is also their center, that is, the Sacred Heart is a point of concentration for its subjects, it is the nucleus around which the human hearts are collected; in other words, the Sacred Heart is a King who leads His subjects to a happiness which is He Himself, the Supreme Good.

That Christ is the King of hearts is a fact that cannot be denied. As a King He was foretold by the angel: "God shall give unto Him the throne of David, His father, and He shall reign in the house of Jacob forever. And of His kingdom there shall be no end" (Luke 1, 32-33). Therefore, the kingdom of the Sacred Heart is a kingdom of all times, over all nations, over all hearts. Our Lord made His appearance to the world as a King. He spoke as one having power, He commanded the forces of nature. He raised the dead, He drove out evil spirits, He cured various diseases. He is served and hailed as a King. Angels appear at His birth, angels minister to Him in the desert, at His command legions of angels would have defended Him in the garden. Even in His passion He appears as a King. In the garden the soldiers and servants fall to the ground, to Pilate He says that He is a King, great miracles take place at His death, as a victorious King He rises from the dead, and as a King to whom all power is given in heaven and in earth He sends out His apostles to subjugate the whole world to Him. The apostles went out and we have it from Christian and non-Christian writers that the kingdom of Christ was rapidly propagated in the whole world in spite of many and great obstacles. This kingdom of Christ, the Catholic Church, has survived adversities from without and from within in the course of these nineteen centuries, and there has never been a time that the Catholic Church did not exist. And today Christ lives in millions of hearts. At every hour of the day there are human lips which pronounce His name, at every hour of the day there are people who pay Him divine homage at Holy Mass or Benediction, in every country there are hearts that remember Him with gratitude, and there is no church, however small or poor, in which might not be found some soul laden with sorrow praying to Him for help, consolation and courage. How many kingdoms have been established and destroyed these nineteen hundred years, how many heresies have risen, and disappeared, how many false prophets rose up and sank into the grave, how many doctrines were preached and condemned as false, generations of men were born and died; but there is one whose kingdom could not be destroyed, whose enemies could not harm Him, who remains the same, eternally, in spite of revolutions, changes and disturbances—Jesus Christ, the King of kings. Many men, the valiant men of this world, tried to conquer Christ the King, but how foolish are men if they think that they can destroy His kingdom. What did it profit the Jews to reject Him as their King? His blood came upon them, Jerusalem was destroyed by the Romans, and the people scattered all over the earth. What did it avail the Roman emperors to rage against Christ? The blood of the martyrs was the seed of more Christians. And what does it profit the enemies of the Church at any time to endeavor to crush her? "For He that dwelleth in heaven shall laugh at them, and the Lord shall deride them. Then shall He speak to them in His anger, and trouble them in His rage" (Psalm 2, 4-5).

Why, then, does Christ reign, and why is the Sacred Heart the King and center of all hearts? Does the Sacred Heart reign by force? Then its kingdom would be of this world. Ambitious kings deluged the earth with blood, subjugated many nations with fire and sword, reigned for a while, and then the subjugated people stood up and destroyed their thrones. Does the Sacred Heart reign by the machinations of diplomacy? Then again its kingdom would be of this world. There have been great statesmen who connived to establish order and peace in their country, statesmen who incited the masses to love for king and country, who did great things for the glory of their nations. Yet their achievements had in the end to yield to the gnawing tooth of time, and their great works broke down. Does the Sacred Heart rule with money and great promises? Then indeed its kingdom would be of this world. There have always been vile men who would do anything for money, but who failed their patrons almost the same moment that the money was not forthcoming.

If, then, the kingdom of the Sacred Heart is not of this world, by what particular means does it reign that we can and must say it is not of this world? This one means is love. Love is not of this world. For, St. John says: "Charity is of God" (1 John 4, 7). But in the Sacred Heart there dwells an infinite love, and this love is the reason why this Heart reigns over millions of hearts. This immense love endeavors to win

[98]

over human hearts to the truth. "For this was I born," said Our Lord to Pilate, "and for this came I into the world, that I should give testimony to the truth. Every one that is of the truth, heareth My voice" (John 18, 37). The kingdom of the Sacred Heart, then, is a spiritual kingdom, which is established and spread and preserved by spiritual means, and the principal means is truth. Nobody is forced to enter into the kingdom of the Sacred Heart: wherever there is a soul in any part of the world that hears and understands the appeal of the King of truth and understands the language of the love of the Sacred Heart, that soul is a subject in the kingdom of the Sacred Heart. The Sacred Heart appeals to the hearts of men through love, and those who are born of the truth, that is, those who are willing to make the truth the principle of their thinking and acting, these follow their heavenly King, and it is to these that the Sacred Heart gives testimony of the truth. It does so, first of all, to their understanding. The Sacred Heart demands of them to believe in God and to submit their understanding to the authority of God. For Christ is the truth, and He brought to man the truth about God and man. For the truth of His doctrine He laid down His life. Therefore He has a right to demand faith of us. The Sacred Heart also gives testimony of the truth to our will. Our Lord is the life. He says that if we wish to enter into life, we must keep the commandments. The commandments are the way to heaven. True, this way is often rough and stony, but the Sacred Heart encourages us, saying: "Learn of Me, My yoke is sweet, and My burden light." Why is His yoke sweet? Because Our Lord Himself carried the yoke of His cross and thereby set an example to us. And why is His burden light? Because He gives us ample grace to be able to carry our cross. Lastly, the Sacred Heart gives testimony of the truth to our heart. We must believe and keep the commandments in the spirit of love. For the Sacred Heart is not a King of fear and terror, but a King of love. Our Lord does not want slaves as His subjects. His Heart is so lovable that all men should love it, because manger, cross and altar are the most convincing proofs of its love. Hence St. Paul exclaims: "If any man love not Our Lord Jesus Christ, let him be cursed" (1 Corinthians 16, 22).

The Sacred Heart, then, is the King and center of all hearts. These two characters depict the real self of the Sacred Heart. It is a King, not of our selection, a King not elected by popular vote or made King by man. It is the King of all hearts because it is the Heart of the King of kings, it is the heart of the eternal Son of the eternal King. Therefore the rule of the Sacred Heart is absolute, and its will is supreme law. All hearts center around this King because He rules by love, He identifies His subjects with Himself and makes their interests His own. He leads His subjects, watches over and guides them. In other words, He is their Shepherd, the Shepherd of their souls, so that the Sacred Heart is in truth the Shepherd King of all hearts, a Shepherd King who is one with His flock and who lives for His flock. To this Shepherd King we owe a heartfelt love so that we can say with St. Paul: "I am a prisoner of Jesus Christ" (Ephesians 3, 1), a prisoner of the Sacred Heart; and, though I cannot comprehend the mystery of its love, yet I will consider it my greatest honor to be a servant and friend of the Heart of the King of kings.

Chapter XIV

HEART OF JESUS IN WHOM ARE ALL THE TREASURES OF WISDOM AND KNOWLEDGE

ST. PAUL, writing to the Colossians, says "I would have you know what manner of care I have for you, and for them that are at Laodicea and whosoever have not seen my face in the flesh, that their hearts may be comforted, being instructed in charity and unto all riches of fulness of understanding, unto the knowledge of the mystery of God the Father, and of Jesus Christ, in whom are hid all the treasures of wisdom and knowledge" (2, 1-3). The Apostle means to say that we can find the fulness of knowledge and wisdom in Jesus Christ. For, whatever treasures of knowledge and wisdom the Christian religion possesses, they lie hidden in Jesus Christ. Wisdom is a divine light by which we see and taste God and divine things. Knowledge is love of truth, together with a facility to discern and act upon truth. When comparing these two gifts with each other, we find that wisdom is the crown and perfection of knowledge. Through knowledge of the revelation of God we attain to true wisdom, we see God and taste Him.

The Sacred Heart is said to be the treasury of wisdom and knowledge. When we consider that the Sacred Heart is the seat of divine love, we understand why all the treasures of wisdom and knowledge are hid in it. It was the love of this Heart that moved Our Lord to speak to us about God and the means to find Him. The love of the Sacred Heart flows into the world in a threefold stream: Our Lord is for the world the way and the truth and the life. Therefore those who study Jesus Christ and His institution, the Catholic Church, find the treasures of knowledge in Him. For, if they love the truth, they will soon find that Our Lord is the truth. But they also will find the treasures of wisdom in Him. For, once they know that Our Lord is the truth, they thereby possess wisdom, for they know God and are happy in possessing Him. In order to find out what treasures are stored up in the Sacred Heart, we only need inquire from the Catholic religion whether it is able to remove all religious barriers that are opposed to the intellect, will and heart of man.

As to the intellect of man, we assert that the Catholic religion alone possesses the treasures of wisdom and knowledge, because this religion alone can heal human doubt and ignorance in religious matters. St. Paul says that all men are able to know God by the things that are made; that is, seeing the world and the things in the world, they must come to the conclusion that there must be someone who made the world. Therefore there would have been no absolute necessity for God to reveal Himself. For men could have acquired a sufficient knowledge of God to lead a life corresponding to the dictates of reason. But the fact is that the pagan world as a whole did not acquire such knowledge, not because they were not able to, but there were such exterior obstacles in their way that they did not know God as they ought to have. For, in order to worship God in the right way, it would have been necessary either that each heathen should have acquired a sufficient knowledge about God, or that they should have acquired it from the pagan philosophers. But every one sees that the first means was absolutely hopeless. For, most men could not do such a thing, either because they were ill, or occupied with work, or because they were lazy, or mentally incapable, or their judgment was not sound. As to the other means, history shows that the philosophers failed, partly because they had erroneous conceptions themselves, partly because they did not want to teach the common people, and partly because they were split up into many schools of thought, and therefore had not sufficient authority. Therefore God spoke to man, and told him how He wanted to be adored by him. He sent Jesus Christ, who said to men: "I am the truth." Being God, He knew not only some truth but all truth, and to show us that He was the truth, He said He was God and proved this statement by miracles and prophecies. He established the Catholic Church, and deposited in her all truth, because He said to her: "I am with you all days, even to the consummation of the world" (Matthew 28, 20). The Catholic Church has existed uninterruptedly to the present day, she has preserved the truth because she is infallible, and therefore she alone can give satisfactory answers to the religious questions that the human intellect may put, and therefore she is the treasury of wisdom and knowledge. But the Catholic Church inherited these treasures from the Sacred Heart. For, it is from the Sacred Heart that the Church sprang forth, and the Sacred Heart in its love for man wanted to communicate these treasures to man.

As to the will of man, we also assert that the Catholic religion possesses the treasures of wisdom and knowledge because this religion can cure our sinfulness. Holy Scripture says that all men are sinners. As enemies of God, there would be no other alternative for us but to despair if we could not be sure that God would forgive us our sins. The Catholic Church can help us, she can give us spiritual life. She tells us that God is our Father who joyfully receives the prodigal son. This loving Father sent His only Son that we might have life; that is, grace. Our Lord procured grace for us on the cross, and it is from the cross that life comes to us, through the sacraments.

It is through the sacraments that the Church heals our wounds. The Catholic bishops and

priests can forgive sins. For, Jesus Christ said
to them: "All power is given to Me in heaven
and in earth" (Matthew 28, 18). By virtue of
this infinite power He said to His apostles: "As
the Father hath sent Me, I also send you. Receive ye the Holy Ghost. Whose sins you shall
forgive, they are forgiven them; and whose sins
you shall retain, they are retained" (John 20, 21-
23). It is in the place and power of God that
the bishops and priests forgive sins, and say: "I
absolve thee from thy sins." It is evident that
the Catholic is better off than any other person
in the world, because he has a visible pledge and
guarantee that his sins are forgiven in the tribunal of Penance. The Catholic also has a sacrifice of which he knows that it is a legitimate
and at the same time the most perfect act of
divine worship. It is Jesus Christ, true God and
true Man, who offers Himself to His Father, and
whom we offer on our own behalf as a token of
our submission to God, our Lord and Master,
and as a propitiation for our sins. This sacrifice
is at the same time the food of our souls; we
receive Our Lord's Body and Blood, and thus we
receive the Author and Giver of life. For, Christ

says: "He that eateth My Flesh and drinketh My Blood, abideth in Me, and I in him" (*Ib.* 6, 57). Hence the Church is able to give us life, because Christ, the Life, is in her. The Church is the mystical body of Christ; He is her head, and from this head the life of grace flows into the whole body. It is evident, therefore, that also for our will the treasures of wisdom and knowledge are stored up in the Catholic Church, because in and through her we participate in the life of God Himself. But the Church has received this life from the Sacred Heart, whose love has become our life.

As to the heart of man, we also must assert that the Catholic Church possesses the treasures of wisdom and knowledge because the Catholic religion explains and consoles us in our sufferings. The Catholic Church tells us that sufferings are one of the consequences of original sin. She points to our faith and shows us that sufferings are to advance us in virtue. Life is a school in which we are to be made fit to see God in heaven. God is a strict teacher, who sometimes seems to be partial. But this is not the case, because God's ways are not our ways, and our thoughts are not His. The Catholic Church gives us examples to encourage us to bear our sufferings patiently. She points to the Man of Sorrows, Jesus Christ, and to the Mother of Sorrows, Our Blessed Lady. When the hour of suffering had come, Our Lord consoled Himself with the thought that He was going to His Father, and Our Lady's motto was: "Be it done unto me according to Thy word." In the night of suffering the Church consoles us with the thought that if even the holiest persons had to suffer, we sinners cannot expect a better treatment from the just God. But when we have fought lawfully, God will reward us with the crown of heaven, He will wipe away all our tears from our eyes. Again we see that in the Catholic Church there lie hidden all the treasures of wisdom and knowledge, for the Catholic Church alone can give us a substantial consolation in our sufferings, because Christ, who is the Way, is in her. This way is the way of the cross, and only by this way can we go to heaven. But the Church owes her power of consoling her children to the Sacred Heart, who loves men, especially when they are troubled and heavily laden.

From what we have said, it is evident that the Sacred Heart has put its stamp on the Catholic Church; it is the spirit of love which she has inherited from this Heart which has stored up all treasures of wisdom and knowledge in the Catholic Church. How important it is, therefore, for us to study the Sacred Heart in order to raise these treasures and enrich ourselves with them, that we may grow in the knowledge of God, and that the wisdom of God, and not the wisdom of the world, may abide in us.

Chapter XV

ST. ATHANASIUS says: Christ deified that which He put on. Now Christ put on, or assumed human nature; therefore human nature in Christ by virtue of the Incarnation was deified, that is, it became the humanity of God. In speaking of Christ, we can use the word "deified" in a twofold sense. The proper sense of this word is, that the humanity which Our Lord assumed is the humanity of God. The other sense is that this humanity was penetrated and permeated by the presence, power and perfections of God.

The Catholic Church, in calling the Sacred Heart a Heart in which dwells all the fulness of the Godhead, derived these words from the teaching of the Apostle St. Paul. In his epistle to the Colossians, he writes: "In Christ dwelleth all the fulness of the Godhead corporeally" (2, 9). These words of the Apostle explain and il-

[111]

lustrate what is meant by the word "deified" when taken in the sense that the humanity of Christ is penetrated with the presence and perfections of God. Since the Sacred Heart is a part of that humanity, it follows that the fulness of the Godhead dwells in it corporeally. The Sacred Heart can be likened to an iron which, glowing with fire, is pervaded by the nature of fire. In a similar way the Sacred Heart is·pervaded by the presence and sanctity of God.

We say of the Sacred Heart that the fulness of the Godhead dwells in it. It is the whole divine Being, God in His entirety, that lives in the Sacred Heart. Therefore, not only part of God, if we may say so, not only some power of God, not only a higher degree of perfection, no; it is God Himself with His whole being who lives there. It is God's essence and God's perfections that fill the Sacred Heart. God who alone can say that He is He that is, lives in it; God who possesses all imaginable perfections in the highest degree dwells in it; God besides whom there is nothing better, nothing more beautiful, nothing greater; God the very goodness and beauty, God the essential light and love, fills it; God the ineffably supreme Being, the eternal Rest and Peace, God, the culminating point of every perfection pervades it with His presence.

But this fulness of the Godhead means not only His presence. Since He is the supreme and perfect Good, He communicates His goodness and perfections to others. Now, since this Heart is the Heart of God, He communicates to it the fulness of His goodness; that is, the fulness of those perfections which He can give to a finite being. He makes this Heart powerful, and wise, and just, and loving, and forgiving, and meek and patient. He gives it the fulness of these perfections; that is, the Sacred Heart has within its limits all the goodness and perfections of God that it can contain.

Among these perfections there is one which makes this Heart so grand: it is its sanctity. This Heart is pervaded by the personal presence and sanctity of the Son of God. The Fathers of the Church assert that the Sacred Heart received a twofold unction: it has the uncreated sanctity of the Eternal Word, and the created sanctification of the Holy Ghost. It possesses the uncreated sanctity of the Son of God by virtue of its being substantially united to the Word of God. And certainly this must be called the greatest grace, the highest benefit that God can bestow on a creature. For, the Son of God assumed this human heart as His own Heart, made it pleasing to God and removed from it all possibility of its ever being stained by sin.

The Sacred Heart also possesses the created sanctification of the Holy Ghost. It possesses sanctifying grace in all its fulness. For, St. John says: "We saw His glory, the glory as it were of the Only-begotten of the Father, full of grace and truth" (John 1, 14). If the Sacred Heart is full of grace, it certainly possesses sanctifying grace. This Heart is also decorated with the gifts of the Holy Ghost. For, Isaias says: "The Spirit of the Lord shall rest upon Him, the spirit of wisdom, and of understanding, the spirit of counsel and of fortitude, the spirit of knowledge and of godliness. And He shall be filled with the spirit of the fear of the Lord" (Isaias 11, 2-3).

This Sacred Heart received sanctifying grace and the gifts of the Holy Ghost in such a fulness which no one else shall ever receive here below. Even Our Blessed Lady is no exception. For, though she is full of grace, we are to understand her fulness of grace in the sense that she received all the graces necessary for her dignity. Furthermore, the Sacred Heart possesses such graces as are given by God to some men, not for their own sanctification, but for the utility of others—for instance, the gift of prophecy, the gift of the discernment of spirits—and it is certainly by such gifts that the Sacred Heart works miracles of grace.

On the other hand, in virtue of this twofold unction, it is impossible that the Sacred Heart could be stained by sin. "Which of you shall convince Me of sin?" said Our Lord to the Jews (*Ib*. 8, 46). St. Paul says: "We have a High Priest tempted in all things, like as we are, without sin" (Hebrews 4, 15). This, then, is the fulness of the Godhead that dwells in the Sacred Heart of Jesus.

The Godhead, as the Apostle says, dwells in the Sacred Heart. This metaphor is to point out the continual and permanent presence of the Godhead in the Sacred Heart. It is a presence which began not only with Our Lord's resurrection; God's perfections were not communicated to it gradually, the created sanctity of the Sacred

Heart and its sanctification was not a work which was performed gradually; the gifts of the Holy Ghost were not infused in the course of time, no; the fulness of the Godhead dwelt in the Sacred Heart before Our Lord died for us; in other words, the Incarnation is the beginning of the indwelling of the Godhead in the Sacred Heart.

The thought that the fulness of the Godhead dwells in the Sacred Heart should inspire us with a holy awe and fill us with profound respect. At the dedication of the temple, King Solomon prayed: "The Lord promised that He would dwell in a cloud, but I have built a house to His name that He might dwell there forever" (2 Paralipomenon 6, 1-2). But we can add: "The Lord has chosen a heart, a human heart that He might dwell there forever." The King furthermore said: "Is it credible, then, that God should dwell with men on the earth? If heaven, and the heavens of heavens do not contain Thee, how much less this house which I have built" (*Ib*. 6, 18)? But, since the Sacred Heart is substantially united to the Son of God, and since the Godhead dwells with all its fulness in it, it is not only credible; it is a fact that God dwells with men on the earth. And if that temple could not contain God, yet in this heart there lives and dwells the Godhead in all its fulness. On the other hand, the thought that the fulness of the Godhead lives in this Heart should inspire us with the greatest confidence. What Solomon said of the temple we can apply to the Sacred Heart: "To this end it is made that Thou mayest regard the prayer of Thy servant, and his supplication, O Lord my God. And that Thou wouldst hear the prayer which Thy servant prayeth in it. Whoever shall pray in this place, hear Thou from Thy dwelling place that is from heaven, and show mercy. For Thou art my God. Let Thy eyes, I beseech Thee, be open, and let Thy ears be attentive to the prayer that is made in this place" (*Ib.* 6, 19, 21, 40).

Chapter XVI

HEART OF JESUS, IN WHOM THE FATHER
WAS WELL PLEASED

THESE words of the Litany of the Sacred Heart refer to two facts recorded in the gospel. After the baptism of Jesus in the Jordan and at His transfiguration, heaven was opened, and a voice from heaven said: "This is My Beloved Son, in whom I am well pleased." With these words the Heavenly Father proclaimed His Only-begotten Son made Man as the Messias of the world. The equivalent words in Hebrew mean that Jesus Christ was chosen as the Messias in the past; that is, from all eternity. The Heart of Jesus, therefore, is the Heart of the Messias, and was as such chosen from all eternity.

When we speak of the Messias, our mind goes back to that long space of time when the Jews and also the pagan world with a burning desire looked for the coming of a Saviour. Messias means "Anointed," and this term was employed by the Jews to signify the one who was promised by God as the King and Saviour to come.

The prophets incessantly reminded the people of the Messias and described Him under various aspects. The prophetic utterances concerning the Messias are chiefly three: The Messias is a great King, the Servant of God, and like to a Son of Man. Consequently we have to consider the Sacred Heart as the Heart of the Messias who appears as a King, as the Servant of God and as the Son of Man.

The Messias is described by the prophets as a King of the line of David. "Out of Jacob shall He come that shall rule and shall destroy the remains of the city" (Numbers 24, 19). His kingdom shall be everlasting. "He [the Messias] shall build a house to My name, and I will establish the throne of His kingdom forever" (2 Kings 7, 13). His power shall be boundless. "He shall rule from sea to sea, and from the river unto the end of the earth" (Psalm 71, 8). His kingdom shall be universal: "All kings of the earth shall adore Him, all nations shall serve Him" (*Ib*. 71, 11).

The Messias is also described as the Servant of God. The prophet Isaias says that the Messias is a chosen arrow, and His mouth is like a sharp sword. "He hath made My mouth like a sharp sword, and hath made Me as a chosen arrow" (Isaias 42, 2). The Spirit of the Lord is poured out upon Him, and His word is put in His mouth. "Behold My servant, I will uphold Him; My elect, My soul delighteth in Him. I have given My Spirit upon Him; He shall bring forth judgment to the Gentiles" (*Ib*. 42, 1).

"He shall not cry, nor have respect to person, neither shall His voice be heard abroad. The bruised reed He shall not break, and smoking flax He shall not quench. He shall bring forth judgment unto truth. He shall not be sad nor troublesome, till He set judgment in the earth, and the islands shall wait for His law" (*Ib*. 42, 3-5). The reason and instrument of His power are the revelation of God. The Messias is a messenger of God. "I, the Lord, have called Thee in justice, and taken Thee by the hand and preserved Thee. And I have given Thee for a covenant of the people, for a light of the Gentiles" (*Ib*. 42, 6). He establishes His kingdom not by force, He does not rule by manifestation of material, earthly power, but by meekness and suffering, and by obedience to the commands of

God. "Surely He hath borne our infirmities and carried our sorrows, and we have thought Him as it were a leper, and as one struck by God and afflicted. But He was wounded for our iniquities, He was bruised for our sins. The chastisement of our peace was upon Him, and by His bruises we are healed" (*Ib.* 53, 4-5). "He was offered because it was His own will, and He opened not His mouth. He shall be led as a sheep to the slaughter, and shall be dumb as a lamb before His shearer, and He shall not open His mouth" (*Ib.* 53, 7). His kingdom shall consist of those for whom He made vicarious satisfaction, and this satisfaction is made for all men alike. "Because His soul hath labored, He shall see, and be filled. By His knowledge shall this My Servant justify many, and He shall bear their iniquities" (*Ib.* 53, 11).

In the third place, Daniel describes the Messias as "like to a Son of Man." The Messias appears in the clouds of heaven inaugurating a new era, not by earthly victory, but by His power and authority to judge the whole world.

At first sight these three aspects of the Messias as foretold by the prophets seem to be conflicting, but in the light of the Incarnation we see them realized and harmonized as parts of the Messianic Office. The great object of the Redemption was, and still is, redemption of the world, which contains a threefold program, expressed in the 44th Psalm: "Because of truth, and meekness, and justice" (5).

From this it follows that the Messias had to have a heart specially chosen and formed for His sublime office. It was to be a heart in which the Father could be pleased. But there could have been no heart that could please Him more than a heart which was human and divine, a heart which is the Heart of His Only-begotten Son. Since the Messias was to be a king, His heart was to be a kingly heart. We know from Holy Scripture how manfully, how untiringly, how powerfully, how uncompromisingly the Sacred Heart fought for truth and destroyed the barriers of human error and doubt. "My kingdom is not of this world," said Jesus Christ to Pilate. "For this was I born and for this came I into the world, that I should give testimony to the truth" (John 18, 36, 37). Love for truth, devotion to the truth, service to the truth—these are the pillars of His kingdom, and where else could these virtues be found save in His Sacred Heart? But, what means does He employ in His battle for the truth? He says: "I am the truth." Thus, love for and service to the truth are not merely some qualities in Him, but He is the truth; that is, the personified love for truth. Where else was the seat of this love but in His Sacred Heart? So great was the Sacred Heart's love for truth that it suffered the greatest calumniations, the severest persecutions, rather than not give testimony to the truth. This love for truth reached its culminating point when this Heart broke for us on the cross.

If Our Lord had the heart of a King, He also possessed a heart suitable for the Servant of God who, in the light of the New Testament, assumes the name of Good Shepherd. To destroy sin and guilt was the task of the Good Shepherd; and if as King His Heart was to be manful and brave, the Heart of the Good Shepherd had to be compassionate and meek. It is needless to say that here the love of the Sacred Heart shows itself in its greatest splendor. The merciful Samaritan, the Friend of sinners, the Helper in all needs, the

Martyr for the noblest cause in the world
few titles express more than enough wh
Heart of the Servant of God, the Heart
Good Shepherd was like. The meek love
Sacred Heart finds its concise expression i
words: "The bruised reed He shall not
and smoking flax He shall not extinguish
send forth judgment unto victory" (M
12, 20). "Till He send forth judgme
victory." This is the third part of the M
Office. He came because of justice.
sorrow and human pain, this great soci
lem of the world, He is to solve. It is H
again that solves it. "Come to Me, all
labor and are burdened, and I will refr
(*Ib.* 11, 28). In what, then, does His r
justice consist? The Sacred Heart poi
cross. Paradox as it may be, the cro
great compensator and regulator her
"Take up My yoke and learn of Me,
shall find rest to your souls" (*Ib.* 11, 29
the Sacred Heart is able to give us suffi
solation to bear with the hardships of tl
life; and if this consolation is mingled
terness, the justice of God will be reve

lars of His kingdom, and where else could these virtues be found save in His Sacred Heart? But, what means does He employ in His battle for the truth? He says: "I am the truth." Thus, love for and service to the truth are not merely some qualities in Him, but He is the truth; that is, the personified love for truth. Where else was the seat of this love but in His Sacred Heart? So great was the Sacred Heart's love for truth that it suffered the greatest calumniations, the severest persecutions, rather than not give testimony to the truth. This love for truth reached its culminating point when this Heart broke for us on the cross.

If Our Lord had the heart of a King, He also possessed a heart suitable for the Servant of God who, in the light of the New Testament, assumes the name of Good Shepherd. To destroy sin and guilt was the task of the Good Shepherd; and if as King His Heart was to be manful and brave, the Heart of the Good Shepherd had to be compassionate and meek. It is needless to say that here the love of the Sacred Heart shows itself in its greatest splendor. The merciful Samaritan, the Friend of sinners, the Helper in all needs, the

Martyr for the noblest cause in the world—these few titles express more than enough what the Heart of the Servant of God, the Heart of the Good Shepherd was like. The meek love of the Sacred Heart finds its concise expression in these words: "The bruised reed He shall not break, and smoking flax He shall not extinguish till He send forth judgment unto victory" (Matthew 12, 20). "Till He send forth judgment unto victory." This is the third part of the Messianic Office. He came because of justice. Human sorrow and human pain, this great social problem of the world, He is to solve. It is His Heart again that solves it. "Come to Me, all you that labor and are burdened, and I will refresh you" (*Ib.* 11, 28). In what, then, does His refreshing justice consist? The Sacred Heart points to the cross. Paradox as it may be, the cross is the great compensator and regulator here below. "Take up My yoke and learn of Me, and you shall find rest to your souls" (*Ib.* 11, 29). Only the Sacred Heart is able to give us sufficient consolation to bear with the hardships of this mortal life; and if this consolation is mingled with bitterness, the justice of God will be revealed in the most convincing manner when the Sacred Heart will say to those on the right hand side: "Come, ye blessed of My Father, possess you the kingdom prepared for you from the foundation of the world" (*Ib.* 25, 34). But so long as we are pilgrims and strangers in this world, this Heart will go on throbbing for truth, meekness and justice, and for those who listen to its throbbing it is the way, and the truth, and the life.

Chapter XVII

HEART OF JESUS, OF WHOSE FULNESS
WE HAVE ALL RECEIVED

" AND of His fulness we have all received, and grace for grace" (John 1, 16). It was with a deep-felt gratitude that St. John wrote these words. For he was remembering that happy hour in which, guided by the testimony of St. John the Baptist, he found Jesus Christ. We also have found Jesus Christ, the Way, and the Truth, and the Life. We found Him when we became members of the Catholic Church, when we were numbered with the faithful. Our Lord's life and doctrine, in short, all that He did for us during His public ministry, permit us to look into the fulness of His Sacred Heart. The works of the Incarnation and Redemption show us that it is chiefly three things that we have received from the fulness of the Sacred Heart; namely, life, truth and love.

"I am come that they may have life, and may have it abundantly" (John 10, 10). This was one of the mottoes of the Sacred Heart. By life we are to understand that great spiritual good by which we are delivered from the power of sin and death, and are translated into union with and possession of God. The Sacred Heart is the only heart that could unite the hearts of men to God. For St. Paul says "There is one God and one Mediator of God and man, the Man Jesus Christ" (1 Timothy 2, 5). From these words it follows that the Sacred Heart is the only Mediator between God and the human heart stained by sin and longing to possess God. For, Christ, assuming the nature of man, was appointed Mediator of mankind with God, to reconcile us to God and to restore the kingdom of God devastated by sin. When we say that the Sacred Heart is the only Mediator between God and the human heart, we mean that no other human heart could by its own power and merits unite the hearts of men to God. For, Jesus Christ says: "I am the way, and the truth, and the life. No man cometh to the Father but by Me" (John 14, 6), and in the Acts we read: "Neither is there salvation in any other. For there is no other name given to men whereby they must be saved" (Acts 4, 12).

There was certainly no need for Christ to die for us in order to redeem us, because any action of His would have been sufficient to redeem us. But God had decreed that the world should be redeemed by His Son's passion and death, and therefore His death was necessary to redeem us. This divine decree helps us understand the fulness of the Sacred Heart, and this fulness is demonstrated by the manner in which the Sacred Heart united our hearts to God by giving us life.

The Sacred Heart united our hearts to God, and thereby we received life from its fulness, in the first place, by way of satisfaction. For us and in our stead the Sacred Heart offered itself to God as an equivalent price for the offences which had been committed against God. "This Heart bore our infirmities and carried our sorrows. This Heart was wounded for our iniquities, it was bruised for our sins. By its bruises we are healed." For it offered itself to God by undergoing those punishments which we ought to have suffered; and because it is a divine Heart, it paid a full and sufficient price for our misdeeds. For, it is the heart of the Lamb of God who taketh away the sins of the world (John 1, 29).

The Sacred Heart united our hearts to God, in the second place, by way of meriting for us. It moved the Son of God to give us a right to supernatural goods. For, Our Lord said: "For them do I sanctify Myself that they may also be sanctified in truth" (*Ib.* 17, 19). The Sacred Heart was sanctified by the uncreated sanctity of the Son of God and the created sanctification of the Holy Ghost that it might sanctify the hearts of men. St. Paul says: "As by the disobedience of one man, many were made sinners; so, also, by the obedience of One, many shall be made just" (Romans 5, 19), and "Being consummated, He became to all that obey Him the cause of eternal salvation" (Hebrews 5, 9). The Sacred Heart obediently offered itself to God that by this obedience our hearts also might become obedient to the will of God and we thereby might merit an eternal reward.

The spiritual goods which we receive from the Sacred Heart are, in particular: sanctifying grace. For, St. Paul says: "Being justified freely by His grace through the redemption that is in

Christ Jesus" (Romans 3, 24). Furthermore, actual graces: "Who has called us by His holy calling . . . according to His own purpose and grace which was given us in Christ Jesus before the times of the world" (2 Timothy 1, 9). Again, other actual graces by which we can do good works and persevere to the end: "I am the vine," says Our Lord; "you the branches. He that abideth in Me and I in Him, the same beareth much fruit. For, without Me you can do nothing" (John 15, 5). Lastly, the glory of heaven: "He became to all that obey Him the cause of eternal salvation" (Hebrews 5, 9).

The Sacred Heart united the hearts of men to God, in the third place, by way of redemption. At the price of the Blood of the Sacred Heart, we were delivered from the power of Satan and made children of God. For, St. Peter says: "You were not redeemed with corruptible things such as gold and silver, but with the Precious Blood of Christ" (1 Peter 1, 18-19), and St. Paul says: "He has delivered us from the power of darkness and has translated us into the kingdom of the Son of His love, in whom we have redemption through His Blood" (Colossians 1, 13-14).

The Sacred Heart, lastly, united our hearts to God by way of sacrifice. The Sacred Heart offered itself to God as a sacrifice. For, Holy Scripture says "Christ hath loved us and hath delivered Himself for us an oblation and a sacrifice to God for an odor of sweetness" (Ephesians 5, 2). "God proposed Christ to be a propitiation through faith in His Blood" (Romans 3, 25).

The way and manner, then, in which Christ saved us reveals the fulness of the Sacred Heart from which we received life. But we also received truth. The Incarnation of the Son of God has this great effect: that God placed Himself in the range of our senses. God showed Himself; and those that saw Him saw God. According to the teaching of Holy Scripture, we can see God by relying on the testimony of reason telling us that where there is an effect there must also be a cause. Since the whole world was made, there must also be a Maker, God. But, since we have also senses, they also would like to see Him; and because they cannot see Him as a spirit, Our Lord took a human body so that they also could see Him.

Now, the Sacred Heart, that Heart of flesh and blood, reveals to us this great truth: that God is love. The conception of God among the pagans was, and still is, terrible and full of fear. The chief object of pagan worship is to placate the gods that they may not bring harm or take revenge. Even among the Jews the conception of God as a God of fear was prevalent. For, since the fall of man it was hard and difficult for the human heart to believe that God could be a God of love. The consciousness of sin and guilt determined man to think of God as the avenger of sin. It is always good to remember that the God of the Old Testament who threatened and who punished a stubborn and stiff-necked generation is the same God who preached mercy and forgiveness, love and pardon for all; the same God who preached the Beatitudes. God therefore took a human heart to assure us of His infinite love and to exclude all doubt that He is all mercy and love toward us. And, so, the Sacred Heart has become for us a fountain of light and a convincing proof, not only for our reason, but also for our senses that God is love and that He loves us. And since He loves us, it is needless to say that from the fulness of His Heart we have also received this love, especially when He died for us and redeemed us from our sins, thus making us children of God and heirs to heaven.

But there is this particular feature about the fulness of the Sacred Heart, that, whilst all the faithful have received from its fulness, it will never be exhausted. The Sacred Heart pours out the fulness of His spiritual goods, and yet that fulness is never diminished. Not only once we received of its fulness; as often as we may, we are allowed to draw water from the Saviour's fountains. For, the fulness of the Sacred Heart flows through the seven channels of the sacraments. If we have lost the spiritual life of grace, the fulness of the Sacred Heart is opened to us in the sacrament of Penance. If, in daily life, we lose through death a friend or dear one, we may stand at the grave and weep until our hearts are broken; over the loss of a fortune or of a good name, we may shed the most bitter tears; our sorrow may be the most intense, and yet all the sorrow in the world will never restore either the fortune or the good name, or open up the grave imprisoning the loved one. It took Christ to find the real function of sorrow for the human heart. One speck of penance, one quiver of real sorrow, and the Christ who was lost to us through sin, the friendship that we have had forfeited is restored again to us. If we wish to receive this life, the fulness of the Sacred Heart is opened to us in Holy Communion. And if we wish to study the God of love, if we wish to convince ourselves that He loves us, the Sacred Heart becomes for us a school of love. Certainly Our Lord could not come nearer to us than He did by opening the fulness of His Heart to us; and if the love of this Heart is not a sufficient proof for us of God's infinite love toward us, then we can have no fellowship with Christ, and we cannot be His disciples, who believe that He became Man and died for our sins.

Chapter XVIII

HEART OF JESUS, THE DESIRE OF THE
EVERLASTING HILLS

JESUS CHRIST having solemnly entered into Jerusalem, there were some Greeks among the pilgrims that had come to the feast of the Pasch. They came to Philip and desired him saying: "Sir, we would see Jesus. Philip told Andrew, and both told Jesus" (John 12, 21-22). "We would see Jesus." These words aptly express the meaning of the invocation: "Heart of Jesus, the desire of the eternal hills." When the Patriarch Jacob was lying on his deathbed, he called his sons and said to them: "Gather yourselves together, and hear, O Sons of Jacob, hearken to Israel, your father" (Genesis 49, 2). And, giving each of his sons a blessing, he said to Joseph: "The blessings of thy father are strengthened with the blessings of his fathers, until the desire of the everlasting hills should come" (*Ib.* 49, 26).

By everlasting hills we are to understand the

mountains of the primitive times; that is, the gigantic, immovable mountains that have been in existence from the day they were created by God. "Everlasting hills" is a poetical figure of speech and signifies the whole creation, all things created. Therefore, the meaning of this invocation is that the Sacred Heart is the object of the desire of the whole visible creation from the beginning of the world.

But how was this desire kindled in the whole creation? Here we have to remember that Adam was constituted in grace. In him there were three perfections: There was the perfection of nature—his beautiful body and his brilliant soul; there was the supernatural perfection —sanctifying grace; and there was in him the preternatural perfection—immortality in the body, and harmony in the soul. But Adam sinned, fell and died. The consequence was that, though man was left in the substantial integrity of his nature, yet he suffers from three wounds: Ignorance in his understanding, weakness in his will, and passion in his heart. Not only Adam and Eve and their descendants, but the whole visible creation was involved in the sin of man;

in fact, God cursed the earth in consequence of Adam's sin.

The world fell into the greatest misery. It is true the Jews kept their belief in one God. But most of them were religious without true piety; the Messias was fervently desired by them, but in the form of a national hero. All the other nations fell into the most shameless idolatry. St. Paul, in his epistle to the Romans, depicts a very gloomy picture about the moral state of heathenism.

Though the aberrations of mind and heart were gross, yet there always remained alive a remembrance of a grave guilt by which man threw himself out of a state of high happiness and great innocence into a state of the greatest corporal and spiritual misery; and thus the desire remained alive of a future Redeemer who would restore man to his former happiness and innocence. This desire is the desire of the whole creation, the desire of man who sinned, and the desire of the earth that was cursed because of the sin of man. We know in what the happiness of paradise consisted. Man's greatest prerogative was that he was a child of God, that he loved God and was happy in this love. For, our first parents had a clear knowledge of God, their will had no difficulty in doing good, and they were not subject to sufferings and death. God conversed with them as a friend with his friend. Therefore, by desiring a Redeemer, men wanted to come in contact with God once more, wanted to know and love Him again, and be happy in this love as the love of the Supreme Good.

Now, this Redeemer hath appeared, the desire of the human heart is realized, the love of God appeared in the Man-God Jesus Christ; and in order to draw their hearts to God, in order to show them that He was their kinsman, their friend and their Saviour, in order to show them that God is all love for them, in assuming a human body He also assumed a human heart, as a most convincing proof that their desire for redemption was going to be realized. And since the Sacred Heart is the loveliest and sweetest manifestation of God's love, we understand that this Heart is the desire of the whole visible creation, because by desiring the love of God, men implicitly at least, also desired to love the symbol and proof of this love, which is the Sacred Heart.

Up to now we have demonstrated the fact that the Sacred Heart is the desire of the whole creation. Let us now inquire into the reasons for this overwhelming outcry of men for the love of the Sacred Heart. It will be sufficient to give one conclusive reason: Man desires to enjoy perfect happiness. Man is created to be happy. But to be perfectly happy he requires the possession of all goods without exception, which is impossible in this world, because history and experience show that no amount of temporal goods could ever satisfy the human heart. Furthermore, to be perfectly happy, man must enjoy all goods forever, which, too, is impossible here below, because, on the one hand, temporal goods are fleeting and perishable and, on the other hand, man must die. From this it follows that the capacity of our heart is so vast that nothing outside God is able to fill it.

This it is that the Sacred Heart wants to teach all men, and thus becomes the desire of all men, because the Sacred Heart as the Heart of God is alone able to make the human heart perfectly happy. For, its message to men is this: God is love, God is the only supreme and perfect Good;

therefore you must seek it if you wish to be perfectly happy.

Hence, the task of the Sacred Heart is twofold: As far as it is possible for us here below, it wants to give us true peace and contentment; and, secondly, it points to God, who will be the perfect crown of our desires in heaven. The Sacred Heart accomplishes its twofold task by reminding us of the words of Holy Scripture: "I reckon that the sufferings of this time are not worthy to be compared with the glory that is to come, that shall be revealed in us" (Romans 8, 18). In this world there is more sorrow than joy, and this is another reason why earthly goods cannot satisfy our hearts. But in order to make us bear with our lot and to give us peace and contentment, the school of the Sacred Heart teaches us that the present uncertain state of earthly things will not be everlasting, but come to an end. For, St. Paul says: "The expectation of the creature waiteth for the revelation of the Son of God. For, we know that every creature groaneth and travaileth in pain even till now" (*Ib.* 8, 19, 22). Since the earth is cursed through man's sin, it bears this curse with reluctance and therefore, so to say, groans and travails in pain like a woman before childbirth. This curse will be taken away when men will be risen from the dead, and then the paradisaical conditions will be restored. The whole creation, as it were, awaits this restoration with impatience; and since the Sacred Heart is the symbol of the love of God, it pleads with it to take away the curse that rests on created things. And if even the whole creation pleads, then man must do so all the more, because he was made to be happy, and for him the created things were made. And although we are redeemed and sin is taken away from us, yet we still have to suffer from the consequences of sin. The earth remains a valley of tears, sufferings do not cease, our will remains weakened and given to passion, and therefore we also plead with the Sacred Heart to make us perfectly happy as were our first parents. But since the present Christian happiness is not yet a perfect possession, the Sacred Heart fills us with hope, and this hope is necessary for us, as the Sacred Heart will establish its kingdom in its own good time. Since the fruit of hope is prayer, we must give vent to our desire for happiness in fervent prayer.

We are still seafarers, we have not yet reached the port of our destination, we still look out for heaven, where our desire for happiness is to be stilled, but it is not yet in sight and therefore we must pray through and with the Sacred Heart that heaven may come in sight. Thus, the Sacred Heart becomes for us a powerful pilot to whom we confide our desire for happiness, and who teaches us how to give the right course to the boat of our life, and who consoles us in the sufferings of this life. The Sacred Heart reminds us of the fact that "to them that love God, all things work together unto good" (*Ib*. 8, 28). If in our sufferings we love God, no storm can destroy the boat of our life; on the contrary, adversities will help us to be confirmed in our hope of a speedy landing. If the Sacred Heart be for us, who is against us? If God gave us the Sacred Heart of His Son as an anchor of hope, should we not realize that hope one day? Therefore let us faithfully stand to this Heart, and let nothing separate us from its love. For if this Heart is the advocate of our true happiness, we shall overcome all sufferings and hardships, we shall come forth victors, not of our own power, but by the power of the Sacred Heart of Christ, to whom all power is given in heaven and on earth.

Chapter XIX

HEART OF JESUS, PATIENT AND ABOUNDING IN MERCY

THE Sacred Heart is good to all men, especially to sinners. Its goodness to them shows itself in patience and mercy. Patience is, as it were, the negative side of the goodness of the Sacred Heart. As a rule, Our Lord waits for a long time before He punishes the sinner, in order to give him time for repentance. But mercy is the positive side of His goodness: He willingly pardons all truly repentant sinners. The Sacred Heart, as the Heart of God, is infinitely patient and merciful. Witness Christ's dealings with Nicodemus, Judas, Pilate, Peter! On the last night of Christ's life here in this world, two men bartered him—one for thirty pieces of silver—and yet he knew Him so well that he could pick Him out in the darkness of the garden and imprint his foul kiss upon the Sacred Face; but Peter, who had sworn a few hours before that he would rather die than deny

Him, did not even know Him on that night of horror. Christ is that patient in His dealings with us. Its goodness is as infinite as the essence of God itself. Since we are finite beings, we cannot fathom the perfections of God. We mentally divide them into attributes, in order to form an idea of the greatness of God. But, in reality, all the divine attributes are one, and not distinct from one another, they are the divine Essence, and since there is only one Divine Essence, Its attributes are in reality one. Holy Scripture says: "According to His greatness, so also is His mercy with Him" (Ecclesiasticus 2, 23). Since the greatness of God is infinite, His mercy is also infinite.

That the Sacred Heart is infinitely patient and merciful, we know from Holy Scripture. "If your sins be as scarlet, they shall be made white as snow; and if they be red as crimson, they shall be white as wool" (Isaias 1, 18). "As I live, saith the Lord God, I desire not the death of the wicked, but that the wicked turn from his way and live" (Ezechiel 32, 11). The Psalmist says: "According to the height of the heaven above the earth, He has strengthened His mercy

toward them that fear Him" (Psalm 102, 11).
When Our Lord conferred on His apostles the
power to forgive sins, He said: "Whose sins you
shall forgive, they are forgiven them." Hence,
they received the power to forgive all sins
without exception.

From these passages of Holy Scripture it follows that the Sacred Heart is so patient and
merciful that it is always willing and ready to
pardon all sinners, to forgive all their sins, to
forget their wickedness and to make no differ-
ence in its love toward them. Who can count
the sinners who approached the Sacred Heart
and found mercy? To Mary Magdalen Christ
said: "Thy sins are forgiven thee"; to the penitent thief He promised paradise; Peter, who had
denied Him, was made the first Pope; and
Thomas, who had doubted His resurrection, was
privileged to put his hand in Our Saviour's Side.
What Mary Magdalen, St. Peter and the penitent
thief did, we all can and will do: when we have
had the misfortune of falling into a mortal sin,
we will arise and go to the Sacred Heart. If the
confidence of the prodigal son was not deceived,
how much greater should be our confidence in

the Sacred Heart. If the consciousness of our sins bears us to the ground, we ought not to despair. Cain said to God: "My iniquity is greater than that I may deserve pardon" (Genesis 4, 13). He had committed a grievous sin, but if he had expressed his sorrow, God would have forgiven him. Judas committed an enormous sin; but had he done what Peter did, he would not have ended as a suicide. We cannot say often enough to ourselves: "The Sacred Heart is good, especially toward sinners. Its love is patient and kind; is not provoked to anger; thinketh no evil; beareth all things; endureth all things; the charity of the Sacred Heart never falleth away. It knows that sin makes man unhappy, and therefore it is always willing to help the sinner and to forgive him that he may regain the peace and happiness of his heart and soul." Of course, it must ask one thing of the sinner: he must be sorry for his sins and be determined to avoid them.

The Sacred Heart forgives immediately. Hardly had the prodigal son confessed his guilt, when his father said to his servants: "Bring forth quickly the first robe, and put it on him; and

put a ring on his hand and shoes on his feet."
In a similar way when we go to confession with
a contrite heart, the Sacred Heart immediately
puts on us the robe of sanctifying grace, puts on
our hand the ring of reconciliation and on our
feet the shoes of actual graces. Hence the Psalmist declares: "I said I will confess against myself
my injustice to the Lord, and Thou hast forgiven the wickedness of my sins" (Psalm 31, 5).
The Sacred Heart says through the Prophet: "It
shall come to pass that before they call, I will
hear; as they are yet speaking, I will hear"
(Isaias 65, 24).

You remember well the heart-cry of David.
And if ever a human being knew and understood
the Heart of Christ, it was David. After two
horrible sins, David returned to his normal self
and penance; and, realizing the horror of sin,
he cried aloud *not*, "Please forgive, O God!";
nor did he utter any excuse for his crime, such
as the strength of his passion. Understanding
well the Heart of God, he simply cried, "Thou
wilt forgive me, God, because my sin is great."
What a reason to give God for pardon!

The Heart of Jesus also forgives willingly.

When we pray in the Our Father, "Forgive us our trespasses as we forgive them that trespass against us, do we realize that our prayer sometimes contains a lie? How unfriendly we are to those that have offended us. The offence irritates us, we cannot get over it or forget it. As a stone thrown into water describes circles which grow larger and larger, so the offence which we cannot forget becomes greater and greater the more we ponder on it. But it is not so with the Sacred Heart. It delights in pardoning us. The parable of the prodigal son makes this truth clear to us. It verifies the words of the Prophet: "Before they call, I will hear; as they are yet speaking, I will hear." When the father saw the prodigal son coming, he did not wait for him to make the first advance toward reconciliation, he did not act the offended, he did not say a word of reproach; on the contrary, moved with compassion at the sight of his boy, he ran to him, fell upon his neck and kissed him. This is exactly what the Sacred Heart does when it pardons a truly repentant sinner. The past is forgotten, the sinner becomes a child of God again, heaven which was lost is open to him once more.

Lastly, the Sacred Heart forgives superabundantly. Sometimes we are not sincere in forgiving our neighbor. Bitter feelings and antipathies have settled in the heart, suspicions prevent us from loving him as we did before. The Sacred Heart forgives in a different manner. For, the Prophet says: "If the wicked do penance for his sins and do judgment and justice, and if he restore the pledge and render what he had robbed and walk in the commandments of life and do no unjust thing, he shall surely live and shall not die. None of the sins which he has committed shall be imputed to him, he hath done judgment and justice, he shall surely live" (Ezechiel 33, 14, 16).

The mercy and patience of the Sacred Heart are infinite in themselves; they cannot be limited by the number and malice of our sins. But after death we can no longer implore its mercy. Our Lord says: "I must work the work of Him that sent Me, whilst it is day; the night cometh when no man can work" (John 9, 4). This thought should spur us on not to neglect the graces of the Sacred Heart, because we do not know when the night comes when we cannot work. To remain deaf and dumb to the call of the Heart of Jesus would be the greatest misfortune for us. Woe to us if the Sacred Heart should have to say to us: "How often would I have gathered together thy children, as the hen doth gather her chickens under her wings, and thou wouldst not!" (Matthew 23, 37). We should be lost if these words applied to us on judgment day. But nobody will be lost who does not want to be lost. Let us implore the mercy of the Sacred Heart whilst it is day, and bring forth worthy fruits of penance. Then we shall be saved and be able to praise the mercies of the Sacred Heart from eternity to eternity.

Chapter XX

HEART OF JESUS, RICH TO ALL WHO CALL UPON THEE

"GRACE and truth came by Jesus Christ," says St. John (1, 17). The riches of Jesus Christ are grace and truth, and these riches were not simply given us, they are the fruit of Our Lord's life on earth, a life which culminated in His death and resurrection. These riches are opened to us, not only by the sacraments, but also by prayer. St. Augustine says: "If you want to obtain justice, become a beggar with God." We can go further and say: "If you wish to obtain the riches of the Sacred Heart, you must become a beggar with the Sacred Heart."

Holy Scripture teaches us of what kind our begging should be. Our Lord in the Sermon on the Mount says: "Ask, and it shall be given you; seek, and you shall find; knock, and it shall be opened to you. For every one that asketh, receiveth; and he that seeketh, findeth; and to him that knocketh, it shall be opened" (Matthew 7,

7-8). This appeal, which gradually grows stronger—ask, seek, knock—is to remind us that we must pray continually and perseveringly if we wish to receive favors from the Sacred Heart. The appeal to ask, expresses the confidence which we must have to receive anything. "Let him ask in faith," says St. James, "nothing wavering. For, he that wavereth, is like a wave of the sea, which is moved and carried about by the wind. Therefore, let not that man think that he shall receive anything of the Lord" (James 1, 6-7). Indeed, the first thing a beggar does is to ask. He seeks to obtain things by words. His words are pleading, beseeching and entreating. The same attitude we should adopt when we pray to the Sacred Heart. The first thing we must do is to ask. It is not always an easy task for a man to ask for alms. Some men are shy, others have become poor not from their fault; and though poor many beggars do not receive what they ask for, many people are unkind to them, scold them and drive them away. These discomforts we have not to suffer when we beg the Sacred Heart for favors. We need not be shy; we are all poor in the sight of God;

and, what is more, we are encouraged by the Sacred Heart in our begging, and therefore we shall never be scolded or turned away. The Sacred Heart says to us: "Ask, beg, and you shall receive." And if we do not receive the things we ask for, or not all the things we ask for, yet we shall never go away with empty hands. For, the Sacred Heart, in its immense love for us, wants to give; its desire to enrich us is greater than our wish to be enriched. Therefore, if we do not ask, it is entirely our fault that we do not receive. For, nothing is easier than to ask and to say: "Sacred Heart, I wish to receive this or that favor; please give it to me."

But, not content with our asking, the Sacred Heart urges us on to seeking. We are to go in search of the things we wish to have. A beggar thinks of ways and means to elicit from the people the things he wants to receive. Poor people, if they are really sensible of their wants, need not be taught how to seek the things they stand in need of. They know how to explain their needs, to describe their predicament, to give a vivid account of their situation so as to arouse pity and compassion and thus to obtain assistance. The seeking for alms, then, points to a determined will to obtain things, coupled with a certain cleverness in the act of seeking. Unlike human begging, Christian begging and seeking is always crowned with success. For, the Sacred Heart says: "Seek, and you shall find." What, then, do we find? The Psalmist says: "Let the poor see and rejoice. Seek ye God, and you shall live" (Psalm 68, 33). If we seek the Sacred Heart, the Fountain of life, we shall live, we shall obtain supernatural life. Again, the Psalmist says: "Seek ye the Lord, and be strengthened; seek His face evermore" (Psalm 104, 4). If we seek the Sacred Heart, we shall find strength to cope with the difficulties of life, and we shall feel strong to overcome our passions. How are we to seek the Sacred Heart? The Book of Wisdom says: "Seek God in simplicity of heart" (1, 1). We should come to the Sacred Heart as men not given to conceit; our manner should be artless, and our mind be free from cunning. For, Our Lord says: "When you are praying, speak not much, as the heathens. For, they think that in their much speaking they may be heard" (Matthew 6, 7). What are we to seek? "Seek ye first the kingdom of God and His justice, and all these things shall be added unto you" (*Ib.* 6, 33). We are to learn in the school of the Sacred Heart how to become holy and just; for it is the will of God that we should become holy and just. If we endeavor to carry out this duty, we need not be afraid that we may be in want of our daily bread. For, the Sacred Heart, which gives food to the soul as the nobler part of man, will also take care of the body as the inferior part of man.

The Sacred Heart tells us to ask and seek. But, as if not satisfied with these two ways of calling upon Him, Our Lord even says that we must knock. Beggars sometimes go from door to door and knock that the people may open and listen to their requests. The knocking points to the firm resolution of man to have at any cost what he asks for. Some beggars are impudent and obtrusive, but Our Lord in the parable of the friend coming at midnight shows us that we are not impudent if we knock, if we make a big noise in order to obtain what we ask for. He says: "Which of you shall have a friend and shall go to him at midnight and shall say to him:

Friend, lend me three loaves, because a friend of mine is come off his journey to me, and I have nothing to set before him. And if he from within shall answer and say: Trouble me not, the door is now shut, and my children are with me in bed; I cannot rise and give you. Yet, if he continue knocking, I say to you, although he will not rise and give to him because he is his friend, still because of his importunity he will rise and give him as many as he needs" (Luke 11, 5-8). This parable shows that even in situations of life where egoism rules, perseverance is successful. But the Sacred Heart is not selfish; it is our truest and most selfless Friend, the Sacred Heart never sleeps, and therefore cannot be disturbed in its sleep; it gives us not only three loaves, but all that we need. When praying to the Sacred Heart, we are praying, not only to a human heart, but to a divine heart. Therefore, let us knock, because our knocking will not be in vain. For, it will be opened to us. The door will not remain closed or, if opened, we shall not receive a negative answer. We shall not be driven away; on the contrary, the Sacred Heart will receive us with divine kindness and goodness, and reward us for our persevering knocking.

The Sacred Heart, then, wants us to be beggars that we may obtain the riches stored up in it. Let us remember this truth especially at Holy Mass. Let us not forget that when the priest raises the consecrated Host for adoration, he shows us the Sacred Heart, which is rich to all that call upon it. The Sacred Heart is then present; let us ask, seek and knock for the benefit of our own souls and those of our fellow-men. Let us remember the same truth when we go to confession or Holy Communion. When we go to confession let us ask for the forgiveness of our sins through the Precious Blood of the Sacred Heart; and when we receive Holy Communion we should pray to Our Lord through His Heart. We may rest assured that such a prayer will be efficacious.

Let us often kneel down at the foot of the cross, and look on that Heart which we pierced by our sins. At the foot of the cross we are not alone with our prayers; they are moistened with the Blood of the Sacred Heart, which continually asks God on our behalf for mercy, reconciliation and peace.

Chapter XXI

HEART OF JESUS, FOUNTAIN OF LIFE
AND HOLINESS

LIFE is a central idea in the Christian religion. Our Lord came from heaven that we might have life. Life is a supernatural good, a good which we cannot obtain of our own natural strength, but which God freely bestows on our souls. It is therefore a spiritual good and consists in this: that we are delivered from sin and hell and have become friends of God. This life is not exclusively a future; it is a Christian's possession here below, though incomplete. The way by which we come to this life is faith in Jesus Christ. It is especially the sacrament of Baptism that communicates this life to us in the form of sanctifying grace, which makes us sons of God and partakers in the very nature and life of God. Holiness is allied to supernatural life. It is the degree of this life. The more grace we receive, and the more fervently we cooperate with it, the holier, that is, the more pleasing to God we become.

The Sacred Heart is the fountain, the source of this life and holiness. It is the spring from which life and holiness proceed; life and holiness originate in this Heart, it is the Sacred Heart that gives rise to life and holiness. The moving power that makes this spiritual spring break forth is the immense love of the Sacred Heart. When we ask what is the nature of this love, neither Divine Revelation wishes nor are men able to tell us what it is. Men know and sense what it is, but they cannot properly define it. Love is the first and most intelligible manifestation of our nature. Love is innate not only in man; all animated beings manifest a desire for love. It is not necessary that men should teach us about the nature of love. From our own experience we know that love is a devoted attachment to the beloved object. Therefore love is a communication of one's own goodness to something else, and this communication often develops into a readiness for sacrifice and self-denial.

The love of the Sacred Heart, then, is devoted attachment to man, and this attachment of the Sacred Heart has opened for us a fountain of life and holiness, and from this fountain life and holiness flow into the world in a mighty stream. Our Lord's death on the cross was the universal and therefore also the only means of our salvation. The principal effect of Our Lord's death was this: that it became possible for every man to obtain life and holiness. But if the Redemption was not to remain fruitless, Christ had to make provision that grace should really enter into the hearts of men; in other words, grace was to be distributed and applied to the souls of men. Therefore the Sacred Heart took an active part, not only in the Redemption as the universal cause of our salvation, but also in the distribution of grace as its proximate cause.

The Church calls the Sacred Heart a fountain or spring, and this metaphor aptly illustrates the important truth that life and holiness are free gifts of God, and the sole motive why God gives us these gifts is His goodness. There are two essential features about a fountain or spring. The one is that the water shoots forth without any intervention on the part of man, and the other is that all who come to drink can have their fill.

In the first place, then, life and holiness are

gratuitous gifts of God, gifts of the Sacred Heart. This means, first of all, that of our own natural power we could never have opened this spring. St. Paul, in his epistle to the Romans, teaches us that the grace of vocation to the true faith is given neither to the Jews because of their observance of the Mosaic Law, nor to the heathens because of the observance of the natural law, but it is a gratuitous and free gift of God, and from this the Apostle draws the conclusion: "So, then, it is not of him that willeth, nor of him that runneth, but of God that showeth mercy" (Romans 9, 16), and he endorses this truth by saying: "He hath mercy on whom He will" (*Ib.* 9, 18). Therefore, if man attains to life and holiness, there can be only one reason for this: The love and mercy of the Sacred Heart; it is the Sacred Heart that gives man something that is not his due, something by which he is uplifted and elevated to something that is above the expectations and claims of his nature. Neither can man merit life and holiness. For, St. Paul says: "If we are redeemed by grace, it is not now by works; otherwise grace is no more grace" (*Ib.* 11, 6). Neither could we have prayed for life and holiness. For, Holy Scripture says: "Likewise the Spirit also helpeth our infirmity. For we know not what we should pray for as we ought. But the Spirit asketh for us with unspeakable groanings" (*Ib.* 8, 26). It is the Holy Ghost, then, who helps us to pray. The prayer of a Christian is not solely his own; the Holy Ghost makes our human words His own. For, without His intercession we could not make a proper prayer, because our natural prayer has no interior connection with supernatural grace; and, although God could give us grace on account of our natural prayer, He does not do so in the present order of things.

On the other hand, the Sacred Heart gives life and holiness to all men; that is, the Sacred Heart offers to all men supernatural life and holiness. "For God so loved the world as to give His only-begotten Son, that whosoever believeth in Him may not perish, but may have life everlasting" (John 3, 16). The world, laden with sin, could not expect to be loved by God, but only to be punished by Him. And yet God loved this world so immensely that He sent His own Son to redeem it. For, this is the will of

God: that all men should obtain everlasting life through Jesus Christ. And St. John says: "Jesus Christ is the propitiation for our sins, and not for ours only, but for those of the whole world" (1 John 2, 2). And St. Paul writes: "I desire therefore that supplications be made for all men. For this is good and acceptable in the sight of God Our Saviour, who will have all men to be saved and to come to the knowledge of truth. For there is one God and one Mediator of God and men, the Man Jesus Christ, who gave Himself a redemption for all" (1 Timothy 2, 1-6).

The Sacred Heart wants the redemption and salvation of all men, but there is one barrier to this redemption which the Sacred Heart respects: human liberty, the most perilous and yet precious gift of free will. The Sacred Heart wishes to give life and holiness to all men, but if man frustrates the intentions of God, he cannot come to life and holiness.

If, then, life and holiness flow from the fountain of the Sacred Heart to all men, what are the means by which we can draw water from the Saviour's fountain? The Sacred Heart points to the holy sacraments. The sacraments have sprung from the love of the Sacred Heart, and through them we come in touch with the love of God. Through the holy sacraments the love of the Sacred Heart enters into the interior of our soul, anoints it with love and gives it grace as a power and help. The sacraments are an immense reservoir in which is stored up all the love, all the holiness and all the goodness of the Sacred Heart, and through these seven channels the stream of life and holiness flows from the Sacred Heart into the world. It is in particular the Blessed Sacrament which is for us the principal channel of that life and holiness. For, if in the other sacraments we receive the power of the Sacred Heart, in this Sacrament we receive the Sacred Heart itself, the Author of all grace.

We ought to adore the wisdom of God in opening to us such a wonderful fountain of life and holiness. The Sacred Heart demonstrates every day what it cost God to redeem us. Many preparations and arrangements were necessary that we might receive grace and have life. Could the Sacred Heart not have chosen a shorter way? It could have, but did not choose to do so. And the reason is because this Heart wanted to show its immense love for us; it wanted to bring home to us how necessary it is for man to be united to God. For, there can only be one real evil and misfortune in this world; namely, to live without Him without whom we cannot live.

Chapter XXII

THE love of the Secred Heart never falleth away. The Sacred Heart in the Blessed Sacrament is always active. "That men may have life, and may have it abundantly"—that is its most fervent desire. Our Saviour procured life and grace for us on the cross. Men were redeemed, and what God expects of them is contained in the words of St. Paul: "What shall we say, then? Shall we continue in sin that grace may abound? God forbid. For, we that are dead to sin, how shall we live any longer therein? . . . For we are buried together with Christ by baptism into death [of sin], that as Christ is risen from the dead by the glory of the Father, so we also may walk in newness of life. . . . Knowing this, that our old man is crucified with Him that the body of sin may be destroyed to the end that we may serve sin no longer" (Romans 6, 1-6). But do those that are redeemed serve sin no longer?

Alas, we know that, in spite of the Redemption, God is continuously and grievously offended in every part of the world: lies and scandal, theft and murder, profanation of the Sunday and many other sins daily provoke God's anger and wrath. The number and gravity of sins daily committed are evidence enough that God has just reason to be angry with us and even to exterminate us. We know how terribly God used to punish sin in the Old Testament, how He sent a flood and devastated the earth by wars and famine. At that time He had not yet sent His only-begotten Son; at that time Christ had not died for us. How much more, then, do we deserve the same punishments, and how much greater must be the anger of God against us to whom He gave all? And yet He is more clement to us than He was to the people of old, because we have something at the sight of which God forgets His anger and is appeased. "My little children," writes St. John, "these things I write to you that you may not sin. But if any one sin, we have an Advocate with the Father, Jesus Christ, the Just. And He is the propitiation for our sins" (1 John 2, 1-2). Christ was the propitiation for our sins not only on the cross; daily does He appease the divine anger in the sacrifice of the Holy Mass. It was not only on the cross that He asked pardon for His enemies: every day He disarms the anger of God, saying: "Father, forgive them, for they know not what they do." When God gave the ten Commandments to the Jews, they were so terrified that they said to Moses: "Speak thou to us, and we will hear. Let not the Lord speak to us, least we die" (Exodus 20, 19).

In the Holy Mass we say to the Sacred Heart: "Speak Thou to us and for us." For we know that the anger of God would come down upon us if we could not offer to God a victim of propitiation worthy of Him. We take the Sacred Heart and offer it to God, reminding Him of that great love which He reveals to us through it, and at the sight of this Heart and for its sake God's justice is disarmed.

The Sacred Heart not only appeases the justice of God and averts the punishments which we deserve. The Holy Mass is the continuation and the renewal of the sacrifice of the cross. On the eve of His passion, Christ said He would shed His

Blood for the remission of sins. Though He cannot die any more, yet this shedding of His Blood is renewed in a mystical manner in the Holy Mass. As the Sacred Heart obtained pardon for our sins both as to their guilt and the punishment due to them, so it obtains pardon for our sins in Holy Mass. The Catholic Church teaches that God is appeased through the Holy Mass, and that it remits even serious sins by conceding the gift and grace of contrition. The meaning of these words is that the Holy Mass forgives sins, not directly as the sacrament of Penance, but indirectly by preparing the way to penance; that is, by exciting us to contrition. The Sacred Heart in the Holy Eucharist wants to touch our sinful hearts by the grace of contrition, and to induce us to wash our souls in the bath of confession.

If we daily assist at Holy Mass, the Sacred Heart is daily the propitiation for our sins; every day we find the Good Samaritan who pours oil and wine into our wounds; and if we have grievously offended Him, He carries us back to the inn of the Church and tells her to take care of us. What a great incentive this truth should be for us to assist at Holy Mass! Christ is the propitiation for our sins. He accomplished this propitiation not only once, no; every day He does so, and if we are lost, it is altogether our fault because we did not apply the fruits of the Redemption to our souls.

The Sacred Heart is also the propitiation for our sins by enabling us to pay the debt of temporal punishment which we deserve for them. Though sin is remitted in the sacrament of Penance, all the punishment due to sin is not always forgiven. There remains a debt of temporal punishment which we must efface either in this life or in the world to come. Of course, by doing good works we can pay this debt. But our good works are often so imperfect that their value is not equal to the debt we have contracted. What, then, are we to do if we do not wish to remain debtors to God? The Sacred Heart opens to us in the Holy Mass the infinite treasures of His merits. The satisfaction which Christ made for our sins is no doubt greater than the punishment which we deserve for our sins. Christ made an infinite satisfaction. If one drop of His Precious Blood was sufficient to redeem a thousand worlds, how infinitely great must His merits be since He underwent so many sufferings and even died for us. Our Lord's satisfaction is an overflowing one, a treasure which can never be exhausted. This treasure the Sacred Heart has every morning ready for us in Holy Mass. We offer it up to God in payment of all our debts. We cannot doubt that God will accept this kind of payment, since He accepted the satisfaction made to Him by His Son. If God was ready to spare the inhabitants of Sodom and Gomorrha if there had been ten just found in these cities, how much more will God be disposed to remit all the punishment due to our sins because of the vicarious satisfaction of the Sacred Heart. If Our Lord hands over to us the infinite treasures of His Heart, and if we are allowed to use them in such an easy way, we truly sin against the love of the Sacred Heart if we neglect to assist at Holy Mass. If the propitiation of this divine Heart remains fruitless in us, it is through our own negligence.

How often is the Sacred Heart the last resource in which we take our refuge. If we were convinced of the truth that the Sacred Heart is the propitiation for our sins, that it is the true remedy against our temptations, sadness, doubts and weakness, we would not expect consolation from creatures that cannot give us true consolation; it would be our pleasure and joy to be present at Holy Mass. The Sacred Heart cannot be the propitiation for our sins without our co-operation. We should have a great desire to be freed from our sins; we should be determined to combat our passions, to deny ourselves and bear the cross of Christ. Let us not despise the treasures of grace of the Sacred Heart. The sentiments of faith, love and compunction shall animate us if we desire to be grateful to the Sacred Heart for the gift of so precious a love which daily appeases the anger of God and daily furnishes us with a ready and safe means of having our sins forgiven and the debt of temporal punishment cancelled.

What a proof we have of the everlasting love of the Heart of Christ through the use of indulgences in His Church! What a power we have in our hands and how easily we sometimes cast aside that power! We may, if we will, have every jot and tittle of the temporal punishment due to our sins clearly wiped away before we face Him. By our sins, we have grasped and enjoyed pleasures that God denied us—for in every sin there is a pleasure; otherwise, we would never sin. There must, therefore, be a punishment which is the offset of pleasure, in order that the scales of God's justice be balanced.

Chapter XXIII

HEART OF JESUS, FILLED WITH REPROACHES

THE prophet Jeremias, sitting on the ruins of Jerusalem and lamenting the destruction of the temple, said: "It is good for a man when he has borne the yoke from his youth. He shall give his cheek to him that striketh him, he shall be filled with reproaches" (Lamentations 3, 27-30). Our Lord appeared in this world, not only as a King, but also as the Servant of God who wanted to bear our infirmities and be bruised for our sins. A heavy yoke was placed on the shoulders of the Son of God, the yoke of serving love. As a yoke is laid across the necks of two animals, so Our Lord and mankind were joined together by a yoke, and that yoke was serving love. Mankind was like a wayward, wild and capricious animal which by its untimely pulls and pushes under the yoke caused Our Lord the greatest discomfort and torture, so that He could say with the Psalmist: "I am poor and in labors from my youth and, being exalted, have been humbled and troubled" (Psalm 87, 16).

Since Our Lord through His serving love rendered mankind such an immense service, we should expect that men would have returned this love, or at least have appreciated it. But St. John says: "He came unto His own, and His own received Him not" (John 1, 11). These words apply, not only to the Jews, but also to many Christians. Of the Jews we must say that they did not receive the Saviour of the world, and to many Christians we must apply the words of St. John the Baptist: "There hath stood one in the midst of you whom you know not" (*Ib*. 1, 26). Our Lord said to St. Margaret Mary Alacoque: "Behold the Heart which has loved men so much, and in return it finds only ingratitude," an ingratitude which assumes the form of reproach.

To reproach a person is to charge him with a fault in severe language. The history of Our Lord's life shows that the Sacred Heart was truly filled with reproaches. We know that the life of Christ was persecution and suspicion. He was continually watched, observed and surrounded by His enemies, and the bitterest of them were the Pharisees. The Pharisees were unjust critics of the deeds of Our Lord, and because they were of this world, they said that His works were sin, that His serving love was a grave fault, and therefore they censured Him, charged Him with sin in severe, unkind language. Whatever He did or said, they always found something to criticize. If He healed the sick on the Sabbath day, He was a violator of the Sabbath. The Pharisees and Scribes who in their earthliness and worldliness used to take out a sheep or an ox from a pit were indignant that He healed people on the Sabbath day. According to the Pharisees Our Lord was possessed by the devil if He worked miracles. One day He healed a man possessed with a devil. His enemies could not deny this miraculous event. Therefore they made use of calumny. They attributed His miracles to the power of the devil. This kind of calumny seems to have been a slogan; for everywhere, in Galilee and in Judea, in the temple and on the streets Christ was blasphemed in a similar way. According to the Pharisees He was a friend of sinners if He conversed and ate with them. When the publicans and sinners drew near Him to listen to Him, the Pharisees murmured, saying:

[177]

"This man receiveth sinners and eateth with them" (Luke 15, 1-2). They could not refrain from passing malicious remarks about His good intentions in dealing with the low classes of the people. According to the Pharisees, Our Lord was a hypocrite if He would not answer their insidious questions, and a blasphemer if He did answer them. When they asked Him if He was the Son of God and He affirmed it, they wanted to stone Him.

These reproaches of the Pharisees reached their climax during Our Lord's passion. His enemies accused Him to Pilate as a man perverting the nation and forbidding to give tribute to Caesar and saying that He was Christ the King. And when He was hanging on the cross, they poured out over Him with a satanic joy the lye of bitter derision and contempt. The chief priests, with the scribes and ancients, said: "He saved others; Himself He cannot save. If He be the King of Israel, let Him now come down from the cross and we will believe Him. He trusted in God, let Him now deliver Him if He will have Him; for He said: I am the Son of God" (Matthew 27, 41-43). Truly, the Sacred Heart was filled with reproaches by the Pharisees. It had certainly been bitter to Him to be persecuted and calumniated. But this was His bitterest cross: that though He only did good, yet His very goodness was hated and turned into a crime by His enemies; that is, by His own people. His own people were ungrateful to Him. But, as St. Paul says: "Christ endured the cross, despising the shame" (Hebrews 12, 2).

Also in our time the Sacred Heart is filled with reproaches. But the manner in which it is reproached is different. Though it was great ingratitude on the part of the Jews not to receive their Saviour when He came to them, yet it is still greater ingratitude when He stays in our midst and we do not trouble to know Him. It was chiefly through envy that the Pharisees filled the Sacred Heart with reproaches. The people loved Him as one of themselves; He loved the people and spoke to them as they would speak and understand. He spoke to them, not as the Pharisees and Scribes, who dreamt of the Messias as of a national hero who would restore paradise on earth, but as a Friend of the people who knew what was good for their spiritual and corporal welfare.

But today it is not through the spirit of envy, but through a spirit of egoism that the Sacred Heart is filled with reproaches. Nowadays men, owing to certain philosophical and religious doctrines, have lost the consciousness that men are social beings, that they are made for each other, that there is a common bond uniting them and constituting them brethren in the sight of God. Many men have lost sight of this truth; like spiders they spin themselves in the cobweb of their own selves and, separated from God, their real life, dig to themselves cisterns that have no water. The consequence is that such men die a spiritual death, the cause being their own selves. The result is a spirit of gross egoism which manifests itself, first of all, in indifference and thoughtlessness in religious things. The Sacred Heart preaches its sermon of love to all men. The object of its sermon is to make them return this love, to make them good and zealous Christians. "The charity of Christ," says St. Paul, "presseth us, judging this, that if one died for all, then all were dead. And Christ died for all, that they who live may not now live to themselves, but unto Him who died for them and rose again" (2 Corinthians 5, 14). It is the spirit of selflessness that the Sacred Heart wants to impart to men. But thoughtlessness and indifference in our love for God and men makes us live to ourselves, makes us cold and unfeeling for that excess of love which the Sacred Heart reveals to us. It is not with severe language that we reproach the Sacred Heart; it is our life of thoughtlessness and indifference that makes us ungrateful and influences us to leave the Sacred Heart alone with its love.

If indifference and thoughtlessness wound the Sacred Heart, selfishness is in direct opposition to the love of the Sacred Heart. Selfishness is a silent and yet loud reproach of Our Lord, who practiced the most unselfish love. The selfish man truly lives to himself, knows nothing but himself, thinks only of himself and seeks nothing but himself. Such a man has no time for the love of the Sacred Heart, which says: "If I gave away My life for you, you ought to give your life for the brethren." The selfish man is averse to making sacrifices for others; the greatness of God's love as revealed in the Incarnation means nothing to him; heaven and salvation are not in the range of his earthly calculations.

But what shall we say if this spirit of egoism takes possession, not only of individuals, but of whole nations? What shall we say if whole nations hate and slay each other in bloody wars? How deserted and pained must not the Sacred Heart feel. Our Lord must feel all the more pained when even Catholics do not appreciate the love of His Sacred Heart. We have eyes and do not see, we have ears and do not understand. He is in our midst, and we, His own, do not know Him. How is it possible that the love of God, the greatest gift of God, should incite us to reproach God for this gift? There is only one reason for that: It is our worldliness that blinds us to the glories of the Sacred Heart. Even now the Sacred Heart is carrying the cross, despising the shame. Its love is so immense that no insult, no shame, no ignominy and no ill-treatment can deter it from leaving us. But who cannot feel that a terrible judgment must await those who wantonly and maliciously reproach the love of the Sacred Heart? For, as St. James says: "Judgment without mercy to him that hath not done mercy" (2, 15).

Chapter XXIV

HEART OF JESUS, BRUISED FOR OUR SINS

THE Sacred Heart of Jesus offered itself as a perfect sacrifice to God. Not only did it lay down its life for us, not only did it shed its last drop of blood for us—it was even bruised for our sins, that is, crushed. The Sacred Heart was crushed under the hands of its persecutors as grapes are crused in a winepress.

Since the Sacred Heart was a victim destined for the atonement of our sins, let us see how it was crused and bruised. In the Garden of Olives the Sacred Heart was crushed by an infinitely painful sadness. The shadow of Our Lord's terrible passion and death began to fall on His Heart. He was alone with Himself and God. All the woe of the coming fatal hours rushed on Him. He knew He was sinless, He realized how precious His life was, He felt what a sacrifice it was to die in the prime of His life. He had come to die for our sins. But death is the wages of sin. Therefore Christ had to die for our sins and to suffer all the other punishments which we deserve for our sins. He also thought of the betrayal of Judas, of the flight of His apostles, of the denial of Peter, of the blindness of His people; He saw Jerusalem destroyed and His Church persecuted and torn by heresies and scandals. In His pain He prayed to His Father to take the chalice from Him and, being in an agony, His sweat became as drops of blood trickling to the ground.

The Sacred Heart was also bruised at the flagellation. Fugitive slaves used to be scourged. But was Our Lord a slave, ill-treated by his master? No, He is our Lord and Master, He is the sovereign Ruler of all things. His Heart feels all the pain and humiliation which the scourging brought with it. Once St. Paul was to be scourged. But he asked: "Is it lawful to scourge a Roman citizen?" But what is St. Paul compared to Christ? To be a Roman citizen was deemed a sufficient reason not to be ill-treated like a slave; but to be the Son of God, to be the Saviour of men, to be the Teacher of wisdom and the Author of all good gifts, oh, no, these are no reasons to be freed from and to be spared the horror of the scourging. What insanity, what a crime!

The Sacred Heart was also bruised at the crowning with throns. The eternal King was made a mock king—was deemed a man who in his folly wants to be a king, the eternal Wisdom is made a fool of and ridiculed, and the Sacred Heart feels intensely the pain and contempt which this torture brings with it. Instead of listening to the Lord of the world and instead of believing in Him, the soldiers deride Him and trample on His honor.

Lastly, the Sacred Heart was completely crushed on the cross. Like a murderer, like the greatest evil-doer, He is hanging on the cross between two thieves, and like the worst of men He dies on the gibbet of ignominy. Again His Heart is filled with pain and humiliation.

When we ask why the Sacred Heart wanted to be bruised so completely, there can be only one answer: For our sins, for our levity, indifference and negligence, for our disobedience, pride and thirst for pleasure.

It was from the purest intentions that the Sacred Heart wished to be crushed and bruised.

These intentions are, as it were, the sweet odor of sacrifice ascending to the throne of God. The Sacred Heart crushed was certainly a sweet odor in the sight of God, and this odor is nothing else than the Sacred Heart's immense love for us. This love was, first of all, a love full of miracles. No mere man could have lasted so long amidst such torments. Since Our Lord was God, He called His divinity to His assistance, not to diminish His pain, but to keep His body alive and to suffer more. No mere man could have survived the bloody scourging Our Lord had to endure, and if he had, he would have succumbed to the crowning with thorns. But Our Lord did not die, He continued to live, because the love of His Heart urged Him to prolong His life. He called to His assistance His omnipotence to render Him able to be crucified, and to hang three hours on the cross; and in spite of such great loss of Blood, He was able to utter a cry so strong that He could be heard by the spectators. No mere man would have been able to endure all these torments, and therefore let us acknowledge that the love of the Sacred Heart was a love full of miracles.

The love of the Sacred Heart was not only a universal love, but a personal one. True, Our Lord died for all men, and all men were redeemed. All men are called to become members of the Church. An earthly king may know many subjects in his kingdom, but he cannot know them all personally. But our heavenly King is different from earthly kings. His death on the cross was a favor done to each one of us. If men bestow the same favors often, or to many men, these favors gradually lose their value by becoming habitual. But it is not so with Our Lord. Though He died for all men, He also died for each one of us with the same love and affection with which He died for all. Each one of us was distinctly present in His mind in the stable, in the garden, and on Mount Calvary. St. Paul says: "He loved me and delivered Himself for me" (Galatians 2, 20). And St. Bernard says: "If there was no other man on earth but you to be redeemed, Christ would have done as much for you alone as He suffered for all men together."

The love of the Sacred Heart was also a love devoid of consolation. We do not find our sufferings so hard if someone consoles us, if a friend has compassion for us, or if we know that our sufferings are not in vain. Hence most parents would do anything rather than see their children starve. But Our Lord's love was different. He could truly say with the Psalmist: "In Thy sight are all they that afflict Me, My Heart has expected reproach and misery. And I looked for one that would grieve together with Me, but there was none; and for one that would comfort Me, and I found none" (Psalm 68, 21). Our Lord suffered, laden with all our sins. Since we all sinned, we could not help Him in any way, we all were enemies of God.

But what was more painful was the thought that for many, His sufferings would be useless because they would not correspond with the grace of God. Now, what is more depressing than the thought of having labored in vain? And how truly unworthy we render ourselves of the grace of redemption if, now that we are redeemed, we continue to sin just as though we were not redeemed. We should comfort and console the Sacred Heart by a good life, and so in some measure supply for the losses this Heart sustains from those who do not want to love God.

The sacrifice of love of the bruised Heart of Jesus, then, was a sweet odor in the sight of God, and it is the love of the Sacred Heart that procures for us the blessings of God. The greatest blessing is this: that we are delivered from the power of Satan, that heaven is reopened and that we can receive all graces for our salvation. Holy Scripture says that Christ died that "through death He might destroy him who has the empire of death, to blot out the handwriting of the decree [of damnation] that was against us" (Colossians 2, 14). But this is not the only blessing. The agony of Our Lord in the garden is our consolation at the hour of death. By suffering in the garden, Our Lord took away the sting of death. Death is no longer a punishment for those that are saved and die in a state of grace. Our Lord's disgrace has become our honor. For, He humiliated Himself that we might become humble, and by our humility we might be great in the sight of God. Our Lord's pains are the cause of our joy, the joy of being redeemed, the joy of possessing the life of grace and the joy of seeing God in heaven.

Let us be grateful to the Sacred Heart, bruised

for our sins. Strict justice would demand that we ought to suffer every kind of pain for Our Lord. But He is satisfied if we are good Christians, who conscientiously fulfil the duties of their state; in other words, Christians who keep the commandments of God and the Church. By doing so, we shall enter into that life for which the Sacred Heart once laid down its own life.

Chapter XXV

HEART OF JESUS, MADE OBEDIENT UNTO DEATH

S<small>T</small>. P<small>AUL</small>, in his epistle to the Philippians, says: "Christ humbled Himself, becoming obedient unto death, even to the death of the cross" (2, 8). Our Lord, compelled by the love of His Heart, renounced His own will and became obedient with a fidelity and devotion which reached their culminating point on the cross.

Being God from all eternity, Our Lord had already made Himself low and insignificant by becoming man, and by reason of His appearance was considered a mere man. During His life on earth He went a step further and made Himself so low that He wanted to take upon Himself the lot of a servant and the death of a slave. The mainspring of this obedience was the love of His Sacred Heart, which moved the Saviour of the world to do penance for the manifold disobedience of man. St. Paul lays stress on the fact that Jesus Christ was obedient, but leaves unconsidered the question to whom He was obedient. Hence we have to consider the obedience of the Sacred Heart in the light of a life-long service.

It is true, angels and men ministered to Jesus Christ from the beginning of His life, but He declared as the ultimate object of His earthly life His vocation of Servant of God; for as such "When evening was come," says St. Matthew, "they brought to Him many that were possessed with devils, and He cast out the spirits with His word, and all that were sick He healed, that it might be fulfilled which was spoken by the prophet Isaias, saying: "He took our infirmities, and bore our diseases" (Matthew 18, 6-7). The prophet Isaias speaks of the Servant of God as the coming Redeemer, who, through His obedience, is to redeem the world. To the disciples of John, Christ said: "Go and relate to John what you have heard and seen: The blind see, the lame walk, the lepers are cleansed, the deaf hear, the dead rise again, the poor have the gospel preached to them" (*Ib*. 11,5). Christ means to say: The Jews are not to wait any longer, the Messias has come, He wants to help the people of God and to raise them through His serving love. "The Son of God," He says to His apostles, "is not come to be ministered to, but to minister" (*Ib.* 20, 28), and "I am in the midst of you as He that serveth" (Luke 22, 27).

The doctrine of serving love is a fundamental doctrine; and when Our Lord speaks of it, He refers to His own example. "After He had washed their feet," says St. John, "and taken His garments, being set down again, He said to them: Know you what I have done to you? You call me Master and Lord, and you say well, for so I am. If, then, I, being your Lord and Master, have washed your feet, you also ought to wash one another's feet. For, I have given you an example that, as I have done to you, so you do also" (John 13, 12-15).

The Gospel is full of examples of the Sacred Heart's serving love. Our Lord's service to mankind is briefly expressed in the words of St. Peter: "He went about doing good" (Acts 10, 38). The blessings He bestowed on the people were of two kinds: Corporal blessings and spiritual blessings. Our Lord served the people by healing the sick, raising the dead, feeding the hungry in the desert; in short, those who suffered from any disease were cured. At any time of the day they brought sick people to Him, and He was always willing to cure them. But these corporal blessings were not given for themselves; through them Our Lord wanted to bestow spiritual blessings. Through them He wanted to win the human hearts over to God. Our Lord compared Himself to a physician. The Pharisees said to the disciples: "Why does your Master eat with publicans and sinners? But Jesus hearing it, said: They that are in health, need not a physician, but they that are ill. Go, then, and learn what this meaneth: I will have mercy and not sacrifice. For I am not come to call the just, but sinners" (Matthew 9, 12-13). A physician's task is service to the human body. Since Our Lord is a spiritual physician, His task is service to the soul. The Sacred Heart was wounded by the cold and uncharitable words of the Pharisees. Our Lord knew that God wills not the destruction of the sinner, but that He should live. It was His infinite mercy that moved the Son of God to come down from heaven and save that which was lost. All men had fallen into the

slavery of sin; no one could call himself just.
Therefore He wanted to bring help as a spiritual
physician, a help that sprang from the flames of
His divine love.

Again, He says: "I am the Good Shepherd."
The shepherd's task is to be of service to the
flock, to serve the flock by guiding it, leading it
to good pastures and defending it from the assaults of enemies; and if some of the sheep go
astray, he is to bring them back to the fold. Our
Lord is the Good Shepherd, and in order to save
them, He knows them all, He knows their good
and weak points. The pastures which the Good
Shepherd offers are the treasures of the Word of
God, the innumerable graces and means of grace
and, finally, the joys of heaven. Our Lord's
loving service is strikingly expressed in the par-
ables of the lost sheep and the lost coin. "What,
think you," He cries out, "if a man have a
hundred sheep, and one of them should go astray,
will he not leave the ninety-nine in the mountains, and go to seek that which is gone astray?
And if so be that he find it, amen I say to you, he
rejoices more for that than for the ninety-nine
that went not astray. Even so, it is the will of

your Father who is in heaven that not one of these little ones should perish."

No weather is too inconvenient for the Good Shepherd, no hill too steep, no road too rough. And when He finds the lost sheep, He takes it on His shoulders and carries it home. The parable of the lost coin is meant to show the same truth; that is, loving service. "What woman having ten pieces of silver, if she lose one piece, does not light a candle and sweep the house and seek diligently until she find it? And when she has found it, she calls together her friends and neighbors, saying: Rejoice with me, because I have found the piece of silver which I had lost." We see, Our Lord's care for souls is scrupulous, He does all in His power to find the lost sheep, and His joy over a sheep which He finds is great. And even though ungrateful men do not appreciate His loving service, in the parable of the prodigal son He depicts the never-ceasing love of His wounded Heart toward the sinner that comes back repentant. Moved by His Heart's immense love for sinners, Our Lord, in this parable, speaks in terms so ardent and so affectionate as to draw all men to Him.

We see, then, that Our Lord's love was a serving love, an unselfish love, a love full of mercy and so irresistible as to move even the coldest hearts. This service of the Sacred Heart reached its culminating point in Our Lord's death on the cross. He became obedient unto the death of the cross. For, the Son of God came to give His life as a redemption for many (Matthew 20, 28). And, again: "Greater love than this no man hath: that a man lay down his life for his friends" (John 15, 13). Readiness and willingness to make sacrifices was the fuel with which the Sacred Heart fed the flame of serving love. Since this love has degrees, the highest degree must be the one which causes man to give away his own life in the service of his fellowmen. This Our Lord did when He became obedient unto the death of the cross. He chose the death of a slave, the crucifixion, to bring home to us that He would not allow Himself to be deterred from any sacrifice if through it He could serve mankind. His office as the Saviour of all men involved the greatest sacrifice for men, because they were so much indebted to God that they could never have paid their debt if

Jesus Christ, both God and Man, had not paid it for and in the place of men. In your daily dealings with people, do you give credit to those who do nothing at all or only that which is easy? Rather, it seems that men give credit for doing only what is difficult. This is true with God and with men.

When meditating on this sublime service of Our Lord, we cannot deny that His example is extremely forceful, all the more so when we compare it with our own little sacrifices which we are so often unwilling to make. If the Son of God became obedient unto death by His serving love, who are we that we should refuse to practice this same loving service to our fellowmen? For, as Our Lord says: "By this shall all men know that you are My disciples, if you have love one for another" (*Ib.* 13, 35).

Chapter XXVI

HEART OF JESUS, PIERCED WITH A LANCE

OUR LORD wanted His Heart to be pierced with a lance that we might have a refuge in all adversities. St. John says "One of the soldiers with a spear opened His side, and immediately there came out blood and water" (John 19, 34). St. John does not tell us which side was transfixed. According to tradition the soldier opened the right side, and the thrust of the spear was so violent that it wounded the Heart of Our Lord. St. John also gives us the reason why the Sacred Heart was pierced. This was done that the Scriptures might be fulfilled: "They shall look on Him whom they pierced" (*Ib*. 19, 37). These words are contained in the phophecy of Zacharias (12, 10). The Prophet says that God will not reject the Jews forever. Together with other nations they will be antagonistic to the Church of the Messias. But, moved by the grace of God, they will realize their crime and weep over it. God will open a fountain of grace for the complete cleansing of sinners. Having done penance, they will look on the Saviour whom they pierced. Seeing His wounded side and Heart, they will mourn and grieve over Him.

From these words of the Prophet it follows that the wound of the Sacred Heart is some holy sign. A sign is something that leads us to the knowledge of a thing hitherto unknown to us. If the Sacred Heart is a symbol of divine love, then the wound in the Sacred Heart signifies that we have access to that love. For the Sacred Heart is both the fountain of grace and our home in all difficulties. We should look on the Sacred Heart which we pierced through our sins. The consciousness of our guilt and the sentiments of true contrition should bring home to us that God turned evil into good. If our sins directed the lance of the soldier to open Our Lord's side, the love of the Sacred Heart wanted to be for us a fountain of grace and a home where we are protected against the assaults of our enemies. Our Lord wanted to tell us that His Heart is always open to us, open to everybody, open at all times and open forever. The wound of the Sacred Heart endorses the words of Our Lord: "Come to Me, all that are troubled and heavily laden, and I will refresh you."

This holy wound not only is a sign, but also a mystery. Many Fathers of the Church seriously hold that, as Eve was made of one of the ribs of the sleeping Adam, so the Church, the true Mother of the living, came forth from the side of the second Adam when He had fallen asleep on the cross. The Sacred Heart is the origin and cradle of the Church; it is the golden door through which she made her appearance into the world. For, the Church is nothing else but Christ, who continues to live in the world and who continues to save us. The Church is the visible and tangible realization of the love of the Sacred Heart. The love of the Sacred Heart wanted to get in touch with the hearts of men and to be united to them. Our Lord accomplished this union by giving us the Church. The Church is the mystical union of God with man; Christ is the head, and we are its members. From this head we receive faith, through faith hope, and through both love. Love is the inmost nature of the Church; the Church is to help us to love God, and therefore she is truly the love of the

Sacred Heart substantiated within the limits of space and time.

According to the Fathers of the Church, the wound of the Sacred Heart also points to the holy Sacraments of the Church. The blood and water which flowed from Our Lord's side are symbols of that life which Our Lord procured for us on the cross, and which flows from the Sacred Heart into the hearts of men. It is especially the sacraments of Baptism and the Holy Eucharist that give us this life. In the sacrament of Baptism we are born to a supernatural life, we become members of the body of the Church, and we become one with our head, Jesus Christ, and this life through the operation of the Holy Spirit flows into our soul. In the Holy Eucharist we not only receive this life; Life itself, Christ the eternal life, Christ the Author of life comes personally into our hearts. Thus, the wound of the Sacred Heart becomes for us the gate of life because the Church and her sacraments come forth from it.

We said the wound of the Sacred Heart is a holy sign signifying that the Heart of Jesus is open to all men. On the one hand, all graces come to us from this Heart, all graces flow in superabundance into the world. For, it is Our Lord's fervent wish to make men happy with His love. Our Lord could not do more than He has done to save us. His Heart is open to us so far as He is concerned. But is this Heart open to us so far as we are concerned? Do we understand the meaning of the wound of the Sacred Heart as a holy sign? If the Sacred Heart is open to us, do we enter into it? We should confess with the Psalmist: "This is the gate of the Lord, the just shall enter into it" (Psalm 117, 20). The Sacred Heart is the gate through which we enter to see God. The just shall enter into it. No doubt, all God-loving souls love the Sacred Heart. But all men are not just, many are sinners, and it is especially the sinners, the troubled and the heavily laden that should enter into the Sacred Heart. "They shall look on Him whom they pierced," says the Prophet. After having realized the enormity of our sins, the greatness of our ingratitude, and the fatal consequences of our rebellion against God, and having washed our souls in the Blood of the Lamb in the sacrament of Penance, we should enter into the gate of the Lord, into the Sacred Heart. Sin has made our hearts cold, empty and hard. In the Sacred Heart we find warmth, and the fulness of grace, the sweetness of divine love and the light of God's inspirations. St. Paul says: "Let us go with confidence to the throne of grace that we may obtain mercy and find grace in seasonable aid" (Hebrews 4, 16). "For, we have not a high priest who cannot have compassion on our infirmities, but One tempted in all things like as we are, without sin" (*Ib*. 14, 15). Since the Sacred Heart knows our infirmities, it has opened to us a fountain of all graces. One of our infirmities is that we do not often enough realize that our life here below is a time of preparation and probation, and that we are called to a higher life. But if we lose sanctifying grace, we cannot take part in that life. We should, therefore, go with confidence to the Sacred Heart, and ask it to give us the grace of perseverance. This grace is absolutely necessary for us; for if we do not persevere in the grace of God, our life here below will be futile. There are also infirmities of our understanding, which through the sin of our first parents became darkened. In order to know what is useful and necessary for our salvation we should ask the Sacred Heart for interior light to perceive what is necessary and profitable for our salvation. No less poignant are the infirmities of our will, which, through original sin, has been weakened. Let us ask the Sacred Heart to move and strengthen our will to avoid evil and to do good.

Thus, the holy wound of the Sacred Heart becomes our home, to which we can always turn in all difficulties, a home where we are sure to find help, a home where we are always loved, a home where we are always welcome. Earthly homes are often broken up, but this home remains forever, because it is built by the hand of God, and in this home there is the fountain of living water springing into everlasting life.

Chapter XXVII

HEART OF JESUS, SOURCE OF ALL
CONSOLATION

IT IS a certain fact that our life on earth is a life of suffering. Even the holiest men were subject to miseries and hardships. The Son of God was mocked and scourged, spat upon and put to death. The soul of Our Blessed Lady was transfixed by a sword of seven dolors. Hence, if the holiest men were made to suffer, we need not be surprised when we sinners must drink the chalice of sufferings. St. Paul impressed upon the Corinthians the truth that to be Christians is identical with being cross-bearers. But it is one thing to suffer, and another to suffer because Christ suffered, and another thing again to love sufferings. To each of these three ways of suffering we can apply the old adage that misery loves company. In its sufferings the human heart looks out for sympathy and consolation. Many men give way to sadness, and try to derive consolation from persons or things that are unable to give it.

Our Lord, the eternal Truth, says to us: "Come to Me." "As the sufferings of Christ abound in us," says St. Paul, "so also by Christ doth our comfort abound" (2 Corinthians 1, 5). They say: It is the supreme tribute of love that is paid by imitation. Since we profess to be disciples and lovers of Christ, we should bring ourselves to love suffering. When God strikes, He also alleviates our sorrow, He sends us to the source of all consolation, to the Heart of Our Saviour. If misery loves company, there is no better companion to wish for than the Sacred Heart of Jesus. He is a companion who knows from His own experience what a heart feels like when sorrow and pain weigh it down. Our Lord shared our lot. He saw a dear friend in His cross, a friend who accompanied Him from Bethlehem to Egypt, from Egypt to Nazareth, and from Nazareth to Mount Calvary. Holy Scripture tells us that He too had to conquer His aversion to the cross. He prayed three times in the garden that the chalice might pass away, in His agony He sweat blood, and when He realized that it was the will of God that He should suffer, He did not throw the cross away,

He remained faithful to His friend, and through His faithfulness to it the world was saved. To this loving companion we should go in our sufferings.

"As the sufferings of Christ abound in us, so also by Christ doth our comfort abound." The widow of Naim was in great sorrow. Her only son, her supporter, had been taken away from her by death, and now they were carrying him to the grave. She would never see him again, and how she would make a living for herself she did not know. God seemed cruel and unjust to have taken away her only son, and she may have found it difficult to be resigned to His will. But, behold, the Saviour appears at the gate of the city. He sees the dead boy and his aged mother and His heart is moved with mercy toward her. Without knowing it, the sorrowful widow of Naim has come to the Fountain of all consolation, she has found a Heart in the multitude that can truly help and console her. The people that accompanied her expressed their sympathy by weeping with her. But the Sacred Heart says: "Weep not. Cease to weep; I will turn your sorrow into joy." He touches the bier, and says:

"Young man, I say to thee, arise. And he that was dead sat up and began to speak." The Evangelist says significantly: "He gave him to his mother." Christ gave her an abiding consolation, a truly abounding comfort. We may be sure that the widow never passed through that gate without gratefully remembering the great Prophet who bestowed such consolation on her.

In our churches there is a small door that hides away the same great Prophet; it is the door of the tabernacle, where the Sacred Heart resides to love and console us. Our Lord's Hands and Feet and His Sacred Side bear the wounds of His sufferings, inviting us to take refuge in them when sufferings befall us. If poverty makes you feel down-hearted, consider if it can be greater than that of the King of kings who lives under the appearance of bread, and whose throne is the narrow tabernacle. If you have to work hard and you find it difficult to do the will of others, remember that the Lord of heaven and earth obeys the priest and comes on the altar at the words of consecration pronounced by the priest. Or are you despised? Remember that

Jesus Christ is neglected, ill-treated, profaned and ridiculed even by many of His friends. Our Lord makes our burden sweet and light. He waits for us to console us, He knows everything that is in us, trying to draw us toward Him. Therefore, let us go to the fountain of all consolation in all our sufferings that the comforts of Christ may abound in us.

The Sacred Heart not only sympathizes with us, but also relieves our sufferings. When St. John the Baptist sent two of his disciples to Jesus, and asked Him: "Art thou He that art to come, or look we for another," Jesus said to them: "Go and relate to John what you have seen and heard. The blind see, the lame walk, the lepers are cleansed, the deaf hear, the dead rise again, the poor have the gospel preached to them, and blessed is he that shall not be scandalized in Me" (Matthew 11, 3-6). Although miracles are less frequent today than in the days of Our Lord, yet we sometimes learn that people were miraculously restored to health, or received favors under extraordinary circumstances, in places where God seems to grant a more favorable hearing to our prayers than elsewhere. It is not without reason that Our Lord said: "Blessed is he that shall not be scandalized in Me." We are inclined to think that God must hear us always and immediately, and forget that God owes us nothing. If He sends us sufferings, we are bound to accept them; and if He deigns to give us consolation, we shall receive it as a gift which God is not bound to give us. Whether the Sacred Heart will relieve our sufferings depends chiefly on two conditions. The first condition is that we must have a lively confidence in His love. As we said before: Christ required confidence in the sick and infirm He healed. "Believe that I can do this to you," He said to them, and it was to the virtue of a lively confidence that He ascribed His miracles: "Thy faith hath made thee whole." Our misery and sufferings give us a right to ask Him for consolation, and to expect Him to be a loving Friend to us, a Friend merciful and more understanding than any human friend, since He is Mercy and Love itself. And yet we must confess that we are wanting in this lively confidence which should seem so natural to us. Why are we wanting in it? Because we know that we are unfaithful to Him, and so often resemble the

Jews, who loved Him when He punished them, but forget Him when He ceased to strike them. But this is precisely the second condition: We must serve God in good days and evil days. We do not seek His consolation because we know that we are seldom on very good terms with God. The root of the evil is that we do not want to know God. We seldom think about Him. We are interested in the things that please us; but the moment we come upon something referring to God, it is unpleasant and we like to turn to something else. If we truly love the Sacred Heart, the fountain of all consolation, we cannot resist the impulse to be near Him; how can we make a friend if we take no notice of him? If we wish the Sacred Heart to console us, we must know this Heart, study it, listen to it and make good use of its graces. And when we know it, we must love it. And when we know and love the Sacred Heart, we shall not only put up with our sufferings; the Sacred Heart will make us enjoy its consolation so overwhelmingly that we shall begin to consider our cross as a good friend who "worketh for us above measure exceedingly an eternal weight of glory" (2 Corinthians 4, 17),

Chapter XXVIII

HEART OF JESUS, OUR LIFE AND
RESURRECTION

THE resurrection of Christ is the corner-stone of our faith. For, St. Paul says: "If Christ be not risen again, your faith is vain, for you are yet in your sins. But now Christ is risen from the dead, the first-fruits of them that sleep" (1 Corinthians 15, 17-20). The Sacred Heart and its immense love are the infallible pledges and proofs that we are no longer in our sins. For, Our Lord loved us so much that by His death He redeemed us from our sins. The same Saviour who died for us also rose again from the dead, so that our faith in our redemption, our faith in an eternal life and our faith in our own resurrection are well founded.

The Sacred Heart is the pledge of our own resurrection and of eternal life in the world to come. For, it is the Heart of Him who raised Himself from the dead, of Him who cannot die any more; it is the Heart of Him who both died and rose again that by His death we might have life, and in His resurrection we might behold the prototype of our own resurrection. The Sacred Heart then reminds us, in the first place, that Our Lord's resurrection is the beginning of our own glorious resurrection. The great obstacle to our own glorious resurrection is sin. But the seal of sin was broken by Our Lord's resurrection. St. John writes in the Apocalypse: "I saw in the right hand of Him who sat on the throne a book written within and without, sealed with seven seals. And I saw a strong angel proclaiming with a strong voice: Who is worthy to open the book, and to loose the seals thereof? And no man was able, neither in heaven, nor on earth, nor under the earth, to open the book to look on it. And I wept much because no man was found worthy to open the book, nor to see it. And one of the ancients said to me: Weep not; behold the Lion of the tribe of Juda, the Root of David, hath prevailed to open the book and to loose the seven seals thereof" (Apocalypse 5, 1-5). This book signifies our sins, which no mere man was able to take away from us. But the Lion of the tribe of Juda, the God-Man Jesus Christ was able to do so. For, He is the Lamb of God who taketh away the sins of the world. He redeemed us at the price of His Precious Blood. For, St. John continues: "The four living creatures and the four and twenty ancients fell down before the Lamb, and they sang a new canticle, saying: "Thou art worthy, O Lord, to take the book and to open the seals thereof. Because Thou wast slain and hast redeemed us to God in Thy Blood, and of every tribe, and tongue, and people, and nation" (*Ib.* 5, 9). Then St. John goes on, saying that Our Lord has made us to God a kingdom and priests, and we shall reign on the earth (*Ib.* 5, 10).

We are kings and priests by God's grace: kings by conquering ourselves, our sinful passions and inclinations, and subduing our whole being to God. We are all priests in a spiritual way by making sacrifices to God and by devoting our life to His service. Our Lord's resurrection is also the glorious completion of our own glorious resurrection. We were redeemed without our co-operation, but we cannot be saved without our co-operation. We may lose the life of grace at any time owing to our frailty and sinfulness.

If we lose the life of grace and die in that state, ours will not be a glorious resurrection. Our victory over the world, Satan and sin began at the foot of the cross, but it is left to us to complete it. We complete it, first of all, by keeping our soul in a state of grace. Christ risen from the dead is our guide and example in our endeavor to keep our soul holy. He is our guide because He is our King. "Have confidence," He says, "I have overcome the world." If He is our King, we are His soldiers. Now, a soldier's first duty is to have courage. The soldiers of the King of heaven and earth are expected to be brave. The Apostle tells us to become soldiers of Christ, and add that no soldier fighting for Christ should become engrossed in worldly concerns. We are also told that every one in the army of Christ must fight a good fight if he would be crowned. When we were confirmed, the Bishop said to us we must become soldiers of Christ, that the cross is our banner, and that we must follow that banner wherever it is carried. But we also know that the standard of a soldier of Christ is very high. Our Lord is not only our King, but also our example, He is the

Lion of the tribe of Juda, who gives us strength in the battle. It is true that we are made of common clay, we are human, and excuse ourselves on the ground that we are human, but we are called upon to be heroes. Our Lord says: "Have courage." Our courage we derive from our faith. For, St. John declares: "This is the victory which overcometh the world, our faith" (1 John 5, 4). We must live according to our faith, and this faith teaches us that Christian heroism is nothing else but a faithful observance of the duties of our state; or, in other words, it is the ordinary works and duties of our life out of which we forge our crown. This we can all do, we can live for God and our soul.

Our Lord also helps us to perfect the life of grace in us by sacrifices and prayer. The Holy Ghost works in our soul and, relying on His grace, we must bring forth good fruit. For, Our Lord says: "Every good tree bringeth forth good fruit" (Matthew 7, 7). God gives us grace as a help to do good works; and if we wish to preserve the life of grace, we must be engaged in doing good works. Since our nature is so wayward and inclined to evil, these good works very often assume the form of sacrifices. We are inclined to trust our own judgment, and would believe only what we see. But Christ said to Thomas: "Because thou hast seen Me, Thomas, thou hast believed. Blessed are they that have not seen and have believed" (John 20, 29). God wants faith, not on the evidence of our senses, but on the evidence of His own infallible word. But this means that we must submit the judgment of our understanding to the judgment of God; we must humble ourselves and recognize that God is infinitely more wise than we are.

Our heart is attached to the world, to the pleasures and riches of this earth. But the Word of God says we cannot serve two masters. To love God often implies that we have to sacrifice things that are opposed to God and to the love of our neighbor.

Also, our will is called upon to make sacrifices. To continually combat our passions is tedious, and we easily get tired of it. We need perseverance and patience. But in order to persevere and to be patient, we have to sacrifice the fickleness and waywardness of our will, and all anger, irritation and disgust must be remedied if we would enjoy peace.

Our sacrifice would not be perfect without prayer. Sacrifice and prayer are the the two weapons with which we make our victory complete. St. Paul writes to the Hebrews: "Christ is always living to make intercession for us" (Hebrews 7, 23). Our Lord is the eternal High Priest who continues the work of our redemption by interceding and praying for us. The Sacred Heart in the Blessed Sacrament prays and intercedes for us. Its prayer should be a great incentive to us to pray for our own salvation. True, we should pray for others, but we need not forget our own concerns. We should do so by making good intentions, so that all the works we perform during the day may be turned into works meritorious in the sight of God. Our minds should often dwell on the great truths of our religion, especially on the four last things. Such meditations will raise our thoughts up to God and bring us near Him.

But the strength to become kings and lions we find in the Sacred Heart, which is the King of all hearts and which made the greatest sacrifices by becoming the propitiation for our sins. If we fight manfully and sacrifice ourselves wholeheartedly, we shall one day hear the voice of the Son of God; and because we followed His voice here below, we shall live and come forth to the resurrection of life.

Chapter XXIX

HEART OF JESUS, OUR PEACE AND RECONCILIATION

To BRING peace was one of the objects of Our Saviour. Angels sang at His birth: "Peace to men of good will." The love of the Sacred Heart is a pledge of peace and reconciliation of men with God. Peace is a present of the Sacred Heart. At the Last Supper, when the love of this Heart was overflowing, it said to us: "Peace I leave with you, My peace I give unto you, not as the world giveth, do I give unto you" (John 1, 27). The peace of the Sacred Heart is the legacy of a deep, joyful calm of the soul which is conscious of a strong protection of God, and which cannot be disturbed by the vicissitudes of this fallacious life. The peace of the Sacred Heart is opposed to the peace of the world. The peace of the world is a parody, a distortion of peace; it is untruth and falsity.

Peace is a state of tranquillity of the soul, and this state is brought about by order. Now, the right order in this world is that we do the will of God. God must be the object of our thoughts, desires, wishes and actions. But the world is an enemy of God, it makes itself God, subverts the existing order, and therefore its spirit is untruth, discord, disorder and tumult. Since the world denies God, it teaches men to be their own gods, and to seek peace in the gratification of their own passions. But our passions derive pleasure from the transitory and fleeting things of this earth. But no amount of pleasure could ever satisfy the human heart; earthly things are signed with the mark of disorder, because they were cursed by God in consequence of Adam's sin. Therefore the world's peace is no peace at all; it is rebellion and revolt against the order established by God. The peace of the world is sin, and no sinner can enjoy true peace. "Therefore do I weep," said the Prophet," and my eyes run down with water, because the Comforter, the relief of my soul, is far from me" (Lamentations 1, 16). True peace we can derive only from God, who alone can appease all our desires in a perfect and everlasting way. But there is only one such Good, God. Since Our Lord is

God, He alone can give us divine peace, which is a true and permanent peace.

It is the evening of the first Easter Sunday. The apostles are assembled in a house in Jerusalem. The doors are shut because the apostles are afraid of the Jews. Suddenly Jesus stands in their midst. He shows them His wounds and His Sacred Heart. His lips greet the disciples with the words: "Peace be to you." The Sacred Heart knows that they need peace. For their hearts are torn with the thought of their faithlessness toward their Master. Again the Master says: "Peace be to you." The Sacred Heart attributes the greatest importance to the apostles' having true peace. Then Our Lord continues: "As the Father hath sent Me, I also send you." The legacy of Our Lord's peace is deeply connected with His divine mission. He was sent by His Father and came into this world to bring men peace, and to tell them that they would be reconciled to God, and that God would give them the supernatural life of grace. Our Lord's eyes look into the future. He sees the world as a great battlefield, He sees many men conquer themselves, but He sees many more wounded and dead. His Heart becomes compassionate and full of mercy. He had told men to conquer the world, sin and Satan. Would they all do so? Would not many be like the seed that is trodden down by the wayside? Would not many be like the seed that fell on stony ground? And would not many be like the seed that fell among thorns? "That they might have life, and have it abundantly" was the motto of His Heart, and now He passes this motto on to His apostles, saying to them: "As the Father hath sent Me, I also send you." Through His apostles His Sacred Heart wants to bring peace to all men. They are to bring life to those that sit in darkness and in the shadow of death; and since death is caused by sin, and sin is disorder and no peace, He gives His apostles the power to bring peace in the sacrament of reconciliation, the sacrament of Penance. The love of the Sacred Heart wanted to give an efficacious means of reconciliation with God to those who, after Baptism, should fall into mortal sin. Hence, St. John says that Our Lord breathed on the apostles when He gave them the power to forgive sins. Hence confession is, so to say, the life-giving breath of the

Sacred Heart, a breath which creates new life in the soul when it is lost by mortal sin.

In order to dispose ourselves for the reception of this peace, we must love God. Love is the queen of all virtues; love engages all the faculties of our soul to love and possess God, without whom a permanent peace is impossible. Love unites all our senses and all the faculties of our mind in God. With a fervent desire to possess this love, we should come to the Sacred Heart. For, the Sacred Heart cannot give peace to those who do not want to love God. For, we cannot serve two masters; and only if we please God, can we receive the peace of the Sacred Heart.

Next to love we require humility. The Sacred Heart is a humble Heart. It says: "Learn of Me because I am meek and humble." We need humility because our uneasiness about earthly things very often originates in a hidden pride. How is it possible to be calm and undisturbed and to have peace with others if we make ourselves the center around which everything must move?

If we wish to have peace, we also need

patience. "In our patience we shall possess our souls," says Our Lord (Luke 21, 19). Our life is exposed to innumerable miseries and adversities against which we cannot protect ourselves except by patience. If we do not do so, we have no peace.

Also, resignation to the will of God is necessary. This virtue is the strongest weapon against all evils and one to keep away discontent and uneasiness. We must often do things that do not please us, and often bear with things we do not like. It often happens then that our peace is destroyed. But if I firmly believe that nothing happens in the world without Divine Providence, and if my will is united to the will of God, my peace cannot be disturbed. That man is blessed who wills only that which God wills, and who sees in his superiors the representatives of God.

If we come to the Sacred Heart with these dispositions, it will give us the peace which the world cannot give. This peace will silence our floating desires that war against the spirit. How many men are never satisfied with what they have. The more they have, the more they want.

They say: I wish this or that sickness did not trouble me, I wish this or that work had come to an end. These wishes are the best proof that we are not at peace with ourselves, that our heart is like a ship tossed about by the wind of our desires.

Peace also protects us against exterior influences. The Psalmist says: "The most High hath sanctified His own tabernacle. God is in the midst thereof, it shall not be moved" (Psalm 5, 5-6). God is in a soul that is united to Him. Since He is the Supreme Good, the sum-total of all that is good, and true, and beautiful, since He is an ocean of perfection, a man who possesses this Supreme Good cannot be troubled, because on the one hand He possesses nothing on earth, and on the other he finds all he wants in the possession of the Supreme Good.

Lastly, only in a state of peace can we work out our salvation. The Holy Ghost who works in us is the Spirit of peace, and cannot live in disorder caused by sin.

Holy Scripture lays stress on the necessity of our having the peace of God. David says: "There is much peace for those who love God's law" (*Ib*. 118, 165), and the prophet Isaias says: "There is no peace for the wicked" (*Ib*. 22, 57). Let us have a great desire for the peace of the Sacred Heart. For, if we have that peace, we shall be satisfied and not long for anything else. For that peace we were created and redeemed, and the Sacred Heart wants to give us that peace as a foretaste of the peace which we are to enjoy in heaven. Therefore, let us often pray to the Sacred Heart: Lord, give us peace, give to Thy servant that peace which the world cannot give, that "the peace of God which surpasseth all understanding, keep our hearts and minds in Christ Jesus" (Philippians 4, 7).

Chapter XXX

HEART OF JESUS, VICTIM OF SIN

WE ARE told in Holy Scripture that as Abraham and his son Isaac ascended Mount Moriah, Isaac said to his father: "My father." And he answered: "What wilt thou, son?" "Behold," said he, "fire and wood; where is the victim for the holocaust?" And Abraham said: "God will provide Himself a victim for an holocaust, my son." Isaac was to be the victim of a sacrifice by the offering of which God wanted to try Abraham's faith in His promises. Isaac was the victim for the holocaust of Abraham's faith.

Several thousand years later, another Son was offered as a victim on Mount Calvary, a Son who could say of Himself: "Before Abraham was made, I am." He was offered as a victim because it was His own will. Pictures represent the Sacred Heart as surmounted by a cross. The cross in the Sacred Heart bears witness to the loving will of the Son of God to die a victim of sin. The divine Victim was offered, not upon an altar of stone, but on a cross. The cross was secured in the Sacred Heart long before the soldiers joined its beams together. "I have loved thee with an everlasting love," said God through the Prophet, "therefore have I drawn thee, taking pity on thee" (Jeremias 31, 3). The tree of the cross is planted in the Sacred Heart to signify that it is an invention of Christ's love for us. The goodness of God and the malice of men joined its beams together to render it fit to carry a heavy load, the load of the sins of all men of all times.

"Christ hath loved us, and delivered Himself for us, an oblation and a sacrifice to God for an odor of sweetness" (Ephesians 5, 2). These words are the true title which ought to have been put upon the cross. For, Christ's love for us reached its culminating point when He became the victim of sin. Sacrifice is the most certain token of love. "My little children," exclaims St. John, "let us not love in word nor in tongue, but in deed and in truth" (1 John 3, 18). To love in deed and in truth is: to bestow gifts freely, gifts that are not prompted by justice or bestowed with thought of return. If I give in order to pay my debts, I am simply an honest man; if I give in order to get something in return, I am not better than a business man. But a free gift is something which is not demanded by justice nor given with hope of getting something in return. The gift of His divine life as a victim of sin was the most certain proof and testimony of Christ's infinite love for us. For, in giving away His young life He had no debt to pay to us, for He owed us nothing. On the contrary, we were His debtors, we had offended Him, and we ought to have suffered His death; it was incumbent on us to make satisfaction for our sins. But He died because it was His own free will; that is, His infinite love. Infinite love must give or die. So great was Our Lord's love that He chose to die rather than not to give away everything He possessed. Hence, He suffered the greatest pains and the most cruel death because He loved us infinitely. Neither did Christ give away His life with the hope of getting something in return. Though He knew that the sins of the world would be taken away by His death, yet He foresaw that many men would not make use of His grace, and be lost. But even from those who would be faithful to Him, He could not expect gifts in return, because, on the one hand, being God, He cannot receive anything; and, on the other, being the Creator of all things, the gifts He bestows upon us are His own.

Christ's love presents itself in a more detailed perspective when we consider that He gave away His life for His enemies. If a friend can give no more convincing proof of his love for his friend than by dying for him, human love surpasses itself when a man dies for his enemy. Even the infinitely great and immense God could give no more overwhelming proof of His love for us than by dying for us. Witness Holy Scripture, which says: "Scarce for a just man will one die; yet perhaps for a good man someone would dare to die. But God commendeth His charity toward us, when as yet we were sinners according to the time Christ died for us" (Romans 5, 7-8). The reason is evident. Life is the most precious treasure man possesses; we all cling to life, we do not like to lose it. We may feel heroic enough to sacrifice it for a good cause, for father or mother or for those dear to us. But to die for his enemy, to give away his life for a person who hates him and has done evil to him, is so revolting to the natural feelings of man that we can safely say that he will not do so without the help of divine grace. Now, what man would not do, God did. He performed what seemed impossible, He died for His enemies. Though we were His enemies, He looked on us as His friends. He loved us with a personal and individual love. He suffered for each one of us, He laid down His life for each one of us.

Christ wants to make us His friends through His infinite love. Shortly before His death, He said: "And I, if I be lifted up from the earth, will draw all things to Myself" (John 12, 32). He will destroy the power of Satan. The moment the Son of God will hang on the cross between heaven and earth, the same moment His glory and exaltation will commence, and His love will set out on her march of triumph through the whole world to make the hearts of men one in the love of God. Then truth and sacrificing love will be the pillars of His kingdom, and millions of hearts will pay their homage to the Sacred Heart, the King and center of all hearts. The tree of the cross on Mount Calvary has spread its branches over the whole world, reminding us of the words of St. Paul: "May you be able to comprehend with all the saints what is the breadth and length, and height and depth. To know also the charity of Christ, which surpasseth all knowledge" (Ephesians 3, 18-19). What is the breadth of the love of Christ? It is the whole world, which is the field of the activity of His love. "Go and make all nations your disciples," He said. What is its length? "I have loved thee with an everlasting love." He has loved us from all eternity, and will continue to love us to the end. "Behold," He says, "I am with you all days, even to the consummation of the world." If we wish to know the height of His love, He says to us: "Be ye perfect, as your Father in heaven is perfect. Seek ye first the kingdom of God and His justice." But the depth of His love is the sinners whom He loved so much as to die for them.

Christ was the victim for our sins also. If He loved each one of us, we all must love Him in return. If we lead a Christian life, Christ will reveal to us the greatness of His love, which surpasseth all understanding. If we are faithful to

Him and love Him with a strong love, He will give us a blessing: we shall go from virtue to virtue until we see the King of hearts in the heavenly Sion.

Chapter XXXI

HEART OF JESUS, SALVATION OF THOSE
WHO TRUST IN THEE

CONFIDENCE and trust in a person are qualities resulting from the extent of faith we place in that person. The more we rely on the integrity, veracity and friendship of a person, the more we expose to him our thoughts, feelings and plans; in short all the intimacies of our life which we would not expose to a stranger. His craving for happiness compels man to disclose his heart to some good friend, and this disclosing brings with it a feeling of satisfaction and new encouragement.

Salvation is the reward promised to those that hope and trust in the Sacred Heart. The joys of heaven, the possession of God and eternal bliss will be the share of those who confide all the intimacies of their life to the Sacred Heart. For, this Heart is the ground-work and the aim of our Christian hope.

The Sacred Heart, this symbol of love, inspires

us with hope. This love is, first of all, the ground-work of our hope. Hope implies two things: A desire to possess the things we hope for, and trust to receive them if they have been promised. We desire things that are desirable in themselves or which we imagine are so. Love is certainly a desirable object, and all animated things manifest a desire to be loved.

Our Faith shows us the Sacred Heart as the most desirable object we can think of. For it is the symbol of the revelation of God's love for us. If the love of a dear friend is able to make us happy, what then shall we say of the love of God, in whom there are no imperfections and who is Goodness itself? God Himself appeared to us with the message that He loved us. He erected three memorials of His love: manger, cross and altar. He became man, our victim, and our food. More than that even God could not do, because He has given us the very best He has, namely Himself. If this proof of God's love cannot stimulate our desire to possess Him, we cannot be called human beings. The Sacred Heart symbolizes those three great stages of the love of God. It is, as it were, the summary of

[237]

that love, and incessantly makes us desire that love by reminding us of the sufferings and death of Christ, who purchased at such a great price our salvation; that is, the bliss of heaven and the graces necessary to obtain it.

Seeing that the love of the Sacred Heart is in every respect desirable, we cannot be excused if we do not place all our trust in it. In our daily intercourse with men, we are prepared to take a great deal for granted. But nothing wounds us so much as ingratitude. Why? Because our own goodness, the best thing we have, is questioned by ungrateful people; and to show them that we love them, we cannot appeal to anything greater than our own goodness, and if this appeal is disregarded, we feel it is useless to give more convincing proofs.

The Sacred Heart is in exactly the same position. If God, the very goodness and love, comes to us and declares that He loves us, and from love lays down His life, and still is disregarded, distrusted and despised, it is impossible to find an excuse to justify such behavior. What is more, such behavior is downright rudeness and a grievous offence against God, who did all in His power to win our love.

And so we see that Our Lord always demanded trust and confidence of those on whom He bestowed favors. St. Matthew relates that two blind men followed Our Lord, crying: "Have mercy on us, O Son of David. He said to them: "Do you believe that I can do this unto you? They said: Yea, O Lord. Then He touched their eyes, saying: According to your faith be it done unto you" (9, 27-29).

"Do you believe that I can do this unto you?" The Sacred Heart appeals to our trusting faith. Trust in a person is acquired by experience. We live with that person, study him and suddenly a flash of intuition tells us that that person is trustworthy. We never saw Our Lord on earth, we may never see Him in the tabernacle, and yet we have an experience of Him, not acquired on the evidence of our senses, or of our judgment, but on the evidence of our faith. The Gospels draw a vivid character of Our Lord, show Him as the Friend of the people, as the great miracle-worker, show Him in His unfailing love in His passion and death. What greater proofs do we need to draw the conclusion that He is Goodness itself, and that we can, nay must, place all our confidence in Him?

More than this. Our experience of Our Lord's character and life becomes such that we must say: "He is our changeless Friend." St. Paul had experienced the force of this truth when he wrote: "I know whom I have believed" I know His character, His Heart, and "I am sure that He is able to keep that which I have committed unto Him" (2 Timothy 1, 12). Since the day we became Catholics we committed unto Him our salvation. When we look backwards we come to realize that, not only have we an experience of Our Lord's character and life, but also of His goodness. We also can say: "I know whom I have believed." Our Lord has been our changeless Friend by bestowing innumerable blessings on both our body and soul; He has been our changeless Friend by guiding us in our difficulties, and by consoling us in sufferings and hardships. These experiences have taught us that He is Goodness itself.

But to banish the least vestige of diffidence and distrust, He has summed up all His love and goodness in His Sacred Heart, and this ocean of love is our salvation, our happiness and bliss if only we will appreciate this love and be guided by it.

The Sacred Heart is not only the ground-work of our hope, but also its aim. Our trust in the Sacred Heart is not only a pledge of our salvation, but is salvation itself. By trusting the Sacred Heart, we trust God. The Sacred Heart reveals to our reason the existence, the perfections, the glory, the beauty and sweetness of God, who loves us so much. It tells our reason that God is our aim, that He made us to know, love and serve Him, and thereby to be happy with Him for all eternity. If we were made for God, we were not made for anything else; and if we put our happiness in anything else, we are useless in this world because we have no aim at all. God could have rewarded our services for Him with temporal or natural happiness. But He did not do so. To show us the greatness of His love, He gave us a happiness that transcends the claims and expectations of our nature. But this is not all. The Sacred Heart also reveals to us that God is our only adequate happiness. It tells us that no eye hath seen, nor ear heard what happiness God will give us in heaven. If indeed the Son of God, in His infinite wisdom, was at a loss to visualize the glamorous beauty of his

Father's mansion, what indeed must be the reality of heaven? Therefore, money, wealth, pleasures and friendship cannot be our adequate happiness, because they are things that are not beyond the reach of our senses and understanding; whereas the joys of heaven are such that they simply transcend our imagination, expectations and desires. But in heaven there is only one thing that can satisfy all our desires, God. He is an eternal, changeless, perfect, infinite and shoreless ocean of happiness and bliss, and therefore able to make us thoroughly happy.

This trust in God, then, is absolutely necessary if we wish to obtain all that God has promised us. If we trust in the Sacred Heart, our salvation is secured. Men place their hope in many things, in health and wealth, in money and earthly goods. But how many trust in the Sacred Heart, through which was brought to us salvation? To be happy in heaven is the one thing necessary, and how little is required of us to obtain that happiness.

Let us trust in the Sacred Heart. If we do so, there will be no more painful contradiction between faith and practice. We shall cease to be earthly-minded, we shall no longer place our trust in things that cannot give us true happiness. Our hope will be in God, in whom no one has ever hoped and was confounded. For "mercy shall encompass him that hopeth in the Lord" (Psalm 31, 10),

Chapter XXXII

HEART OF JESUS, HOPE OF THOSE WHO
DIE IN THEE

WHEN thinking of the hour of our death, we picture to ourselves those fearful and so often decisive circumstances which will accompany our dying. But we should not forget that Our Lord by His death has taken away the sting of death. Holy Scripture says: "With him that feareth the Lord, it shall go well in the latter end, and in the day of his death he shall be blessed" (Ecclesiasticus 1, 13). The sting of death is sin, the unforgiven, deadly guilt of mortal sin with which a man enters into eternity and appears before his Judge. Unless this guilt is taken away and mortal sin effeaced in the tribunal of Penance, we cannot die in the love of the Sacred Heart. But even if we are reconciled with God on our death-bed, the devil will make his last and biggest effort at the hour of our death to make us unhappy for all eternity. The remembrance of our past sins may trouble us, the thought of the instant judgment may frighten us. To escape the throes of despair, we need someone who can defend us before the tribunal of Jesus Christ; and paradox as it may seem, the Church points to the very Heart of the Judge as our Advocate at the hour of our death.

"If any man sin," says St. John, "we have an Advocate with the Father, Jesus Christ, the Just" (1 John 2, 1). Since Jesus Christ is our Judge and Advocate at the same time, it stands to reason that He is a Judge only for those who are so unfortunate as not to want to love Him, and who reject His grace even at the hour of their death. But He is the Advocate of those who die in His grace, but are troubled by fear and anxiety in that decisive hour. Jesus Christ is our Advocate through His Sacred Heart, which so fervently desires our salvation, and therefore the Sacred Heart is our hope in the hour of our death, it is our Advocate who defends us before the Judge.

An advocate is a man who pleads the cause of another in a court of law and defends his case by arguments. An advocate is expected to know the law and to be diligent in bringing forth such arguments as may prove the innocence or the right of his client. The Sacred Heart is our Advocate in a cause the issue of which is of the greatest importance. For, at the hour of our death our eternal happiness is at stake. We are to appear before a Judge who knows the law very well, because He is the supreme Lawgiver. We have to appear before a Judge who is all-wise, who knows even our most secret thoughts. We have to give an account of our life to a Judge who is Justice itself, and therefore is absolutely incorruptible, and will pass sentence on us exactly as we deserve it. Therefore we need an Advocate who is able to plead with God.

This Advocate is Jesus Christ, of whom St. Paul says: "He is a High Priest, holy, innocent, undefiled, separated from sinners, and made higher than the heavens" (Hebrews 7, 26). Since our Advocate is the God-Man Jesus Christ, we can joyfully place all our confidence in His Sacred Heart. If at any time, it is at the hour of death that we need a faithful Friend. A human advocate is bound to examine the case of his client and to tell him if there is any hope of success. The Sacred Heart examined our case at the Incarnation, and its verdict was: They are to have life, and have it abundantly. When Our Lord appeared, the world was lying in sin and, humanly speaking, there was no hope of mankind's ever entering into heaven. The world was in darkness, man did not know who made him and why he was on earth. The Sacred Heart brought light into the world, because Our Lord is the Light of the world. He found that man had gone astray. He brought him back by saying that He was the way. He found the human heart engrossed in worldly things, He saw it hunting after values that are merely of this world. He showed it higher values by saying that He was the truth.

But to make our cause thoroughly successful He died for us, "blotting out the handwriting of the decree [of damnation] that was against us, which was contrary to us" (Colossians 2, 14). In other words, through Our Lord's death we became just, we were made children of God and became pleasing to Him through grace. Therefore the Sacred Heart is our hope, because at the hour of our death it inspires us with the thought that if we die as children of God we cannot be lost. The love of the Sacred Heart which it bore for us in its passion is the infallible guarantee that, no matter how often and grievously we may have sinned in the past, if we die in the love and grace of God we shall be received by Him as His dear children. This thought, then, is a very strong consolation for us at the hour of our death. If we die in the love of the Sacred Heart, we may indeed have to pass through the sufferings of purgatory, but we shall not be lost.

In the second place, we expect a human advocate to employ every possible diligence in bringing forth such arguments as may prove the innocence or the right of his client. Through Our Lord's death our case is at least half won. For, if we wish, we can be saved by making good use of the means of grace which Our Lord procured for us. St. Paul writes: "He is able also to save them that come to God by Him; always living to make intercession for us" (Hebrews 7, 25).

Our devotion to the Sacred Heart is the best preparation for a happy death. On the one hand, we do not know when God will call us out of this life; it would therefore be presumptuous to be careless and postpone our preparation for the hour of death. On the other hand, we are commanded to love God with all our heart. But Our Lord is able to save us, for He has given us so many means of loving Him. He has taught us to pray, He has given us the sacraments, our sins can be forgiven in the sacrament of Penance, and Holy Communion is a bulwark against sin and a fortress of life. He has given us the Holy Ghost to work in us, He gives us many inspirations, He even appointed men to help us: parents, priests, and teachers. He is the eternal High Priest who prays for us in heaven. Therefore, if we wish to die in the love of the Sacred Heart, it is while we have time that we must prepare ourselves for a happy death. The life of a Christian should be a copy of the life of Christ; and how ungrateful and foolish we should be if we wanted to prepare ourselves just at the last minute. To die well is the greatest art, and this art cannot be learnt at the hour of death; it takes a lifetime to learn it. We should commend our soul to God every night before we go to bed. For, we do not know what may happen to us during the night. We should commend our soul to God before every confession. We should confess our sins as if it were our last confession, and as if our next confession were to take place before the judgment seat of God. Lastly, we should commend our soul to God before every Holy Communion. The Holy Communion we are about to receive may be the last of our life, our Viaticum. If we keep these practices, we shall surely die in the love of the Sacred Heart.

Since we have such a great and powerful Advocate at the hour of our death, it is more than just that we should thank God for such a grace. Our gratitude will be the greater, the more we realize by faith how important the hour of death is. It is certainly not a trifling thing to know or not to know whether we shall be happy for all eternity, or unhappy in hell. Another thought worth remembering is that Our Lord took upon Himself all His sufferings that we might have a happy death. Hence, let us not sin against the immense love of the Sacred Heart, which wants to be our hope at the hour of death. This love simply transcends everything that God has done for us, it is the culminating point of His works;

and if we despised this excess of love, should we be surprised if God punished us by not giving us the Sacred Heart as an Advocate at the hour of our death? For, fearful are the words of St. Paul: "It is impossible for those who were once illuminated, have tasted also the heavenly gifts, and were made partakers of the Holy Ghost, have moreover tested the good work of God and the power of the world to come and are fallen away, to be renewed again to penance, crucifying again to themselves the Son of God, and making Him a mockery" (Hebrews 6, 4-6).

"What do you think of Christ?" Our every act and thought, our hopes and desires are answering that question.

Chapter XXXIII

HEART OF JESUS, DELIGHT OF ALL
THE SAINTS

OUR reflections on the Sacred Heart come to a close in this meditation. The Litany of the Sacred Heart of Jesus has shown us the length, and the breadth, the height and the depth of the infinite love of Our Saviour's Heart. We have realized that, since this Heart loves us so infinitely, Our Lord does not demand too much when He says: "Thou shalt love the Lord thy God with thy whole heart, with thy whole soul, with all thy strength, and with all thy mind" (Luke 10, 27). But the question arises: Is it possible for us to love the Sacred Heart as the law of Christ prescribes? The answer is: On this earth we can love the Sacred Heart only to a certain extent. We can love it with our whole heart by refusing to love anything which is opposed to the love of God; we can love it with all our mind by denying no truth that comes from it; we can love it with our whole strength by devoting all the energies of our being to its love. But we know how we have to struggle to remain in this love, how easily we offend this noblest of hearts, and how ungratefully we forget its love. Therefore, only in heaven can we love the Sacred Heart fully as the law prescribes. In heaven alone can we love the Sacred Heart with our whole heart, with our whole soul and with all our strength.

There is something consoling in the truth that the Sacred Heart is the delight of all the saints, and that it will be our delight when we are safe in heaven. For, if God alone can be our perfect happiness, and if on this earth we are always in danger of losing that happiness, how happy we shall be when the Sacred Heart will make us drink of the torrent of its love and all danger of losing this love will forever be eliminated. The Sacred Heart will be our delight, because it is the Heart of Him who says: "Behold, I make all things new" (Apocalypse 21, 5).

The Sacred Heart will give us a new happiness, the happiness of heaven. If we sincerely love this Heart here below, we are not merely holier but happier even in our sufferings and trials. But this happiness is not perfect and complete. St. Paul says: "If in this life only we have hope in Christ, we are of all men most miserable" (1 Corinthians 15, 19). For, it would avail us nothing to love the Sacred Heart if it could not give us what we so ardently crave for; namely, everlasting happiness. In heaven we shall possess the perfect love of God, which alone can make us perfectly content. On earth it is the aim of the Sacred Heart to prepare us for that perfect love. In heaven we shall be inebriated with the plenty of God's house, we shall drink of the torrent of God's joy. We shall have a new heart, because we shall truly be God's children and His heirs. Our souls will be free from all stains, they will possess all the perfections Adam and Eve had before the fall. The powers of the soul will no longer be darkened and debilitated, and therefore we shall see God as He is, and love Him as we wish, and this will constitute our eternal delight and pleasure.

The Sacred Heart will also give us a new peace, the peace of heaven. We know from experience how hard it is sometimes to let our soul enjoy the peace it requires in order to do the will of God. Sin is the enemy of this peace. We sin because we are proud. But pride destroys our peace because it subverts the right order: we prefer ourselves to God. We sin because we are not patient. Impatience is inimical to the peace of our soul because destructive of the right order: our life is exposed to many miseries which tempt us to lose our temper. But the right order is that we should control our passions. We sin because we are not resigned to God's will, and the want of resignation undermines our peace. We forget that Divine Providence watches over us. We sin because we do not love our neighbor as we ought. But the right order is to love him as ourselves. From all this it follows that perfect peace cannot be found on earth. But the peace which we shall enjoy in heaven is that peace which surpasses our understanding. We shall be united to God, the Supreme Good; He will draw us to Himself, and will never let us go. And since in heaven we find the absolute, complete and perpetual possession of God whom we love, and nothing can separate us from Him, we shall be in undisturbed possession of the Supreme Good, and therefore have eternal peace.

Furthermore, the Sacred Heart will give us a new joy, the joy of heaven. Holy Scripture says of earthly joy: "Laughter shall be mingled with sorrow, and mourning taketh hold of the end of joy" (Proverbs 14, 13). There is more sorrow than joy in this world. The universal law is not joy, but progress. It is the will of God that, above all things, we should develop the powers of our soul. This life is not a playground, but a school where God trains us for heaven. If God deems it necessary, He chastises us that we may reach heaven well educated and well trained. These truths explain why there is more sorrow than joy on earth. Christ says: "Amen, amen, I say to you, that you shall lament and weep, but the world shall rejoice; you shall be made sorrowful, but your surrow shall be turned into joy. You now indeed have sorrow, but I will see you again, and your heart shall rejoice, and your joy no man shall take away from you" (John 16, 20 and 22). In heaven the Sacred Heart will turn our sorrow into joy, a joy which will never be taken away from us. In heaven there are joys which we cannot even imagine. They are divine joys. God will say to us: Enter thou into the joy of thy Lord. Hence we shall partake of the joy which God, the Supreme Good, possesses.

Lastly, the Sacred Heart will give us a new life, the everlasting life of heaven. Time will cease to exist, we shall speak no more of yesterday or tomorrow; our life in heaven will be an everlasting today. Heaven would cease to be heaven if there was any fear that it could end. But no such fear shall ever trouble us, our happiness will never cease, will never be interrupted for a single moment, we shall be always with the Lord. Time passes because it is composed of parts, but eternity cannot pass because it has no parts. Hence St. Peter says: "Of this one thing be not ignorant, my beloved, that one day with the Lord is as a thousand years, and a thousand years as one day" (2 Peter 3, 8).

Such, then, are the things which the Sacred Heart will make new. We have seen the glories of the Sacred Heart, but only through a looking glass and in dark manner. The more we contemplate its glories, the more we feel compelled to exclaim with the Psalmist: "What shall I render to the Lord for all the things that He hath rendered to me? I will pay my vows to the

Lord before all His people" (Psalm 115, 12, 14). Let us pay to the Sacred Heart our Baptismal Vows, let us carry out the promises we made to God on the day of our Baptism. We belong to the Sacred Heart body and soul. It has loved and still loves us. For "you are bought with a great price. Glorify and bear God in your body" (1 Corinthians 6, 19-20). If our life is a service of the Sacred Heart, if we return the love of this Heart, if we are its worshipers in spirit and truth, it will enable us to realize the value of the soul, teach us the supernatural power of our religion and, above all, it will teach us to live more and more the life of Christ on earth; and after we have become like to Him, it will be our eternal delight in heaven.

PRINTED BY BENZIGER BROTHERS, NEW YORK